From Despair to Hope

A Mother's Journey

BONNIE RAFFAELE

Where to get copies of this book.

For ordering information contact Bonnie Raffaele at BlueBird Publishing or search Amazon.com, Amazon's Kindle E-books and CreateSpace.com for a hard copy of this book.

From Dispair to Hope
A Mother's Journey

BONNIE RAFFAELE

BLUEBIRD PUBLISHING

SAULT STE. MARIE, MICHIGAN

From Despair to Hope
A Mother's Journey

COPYRIGHTS @ 2013 BY BONNIE RAFFAELE

All rights Reserved. No part of this publication may
be reproduced in any form without the prior
permission of Bonnie Raffaele
except for short quotations for review reference.

Address all Correspondence to:

BlueBird Publishing
Sault Ste. Marie, MI 49783
E-mail: bonnie@thekdrchallenge.com
Website: www.thekdrchallenge.com

Dedication

To my Kelsey:

Thank you

for raising your hand.

Thank You

A special thank you to Kenn Filkins for all his work on this book. It would not be possible without him.

My thanks also to Adam Raffaele for creating the blue birds.

I would also like to thank my husband, Ron, for putting up with me and supporting me through all of this.

And last, but not least, my beautiful daughter Courtney. I love her more than words can say. My life would be nothing without her.

. . . To the moon and back a BILLION times . . .

Forward

On January 24, 2010 my life as I knew it was gone. A parent's worst nightmare was happening to me. How was I supposed to get through this? What was I supposed to do?

Two years later I found myself asking God, "What do you want me to do?" In order for me to find out what I was supposed to do, I needed to figure out how I got from the worst day of my life to where I am today.

Four words and four scriptures kept coming up over the last couple years.

• Believe
Mark 9:23 And Jesus said to him, "If You can?' All things are possible to him who believes."

• Trust
Proverbs 3:5 "Trust in the Lord with all your heart and lean not on your own understanding."

• Purpose
Romans 8:28, "And we know that in all things God works for the good of those who love him, who have been called according to his purpose".

• Strength
Philippians 4:13 "I can do all things through Christ who gives me strength"

This is the story of my journey. How my daughter raised her hand and led not just others to Jesus, but how she led me closer to Christ.

I can do all things
through Christ
who give me
strength.

Philippians 4:13 (NASB)

Table of Contents

Forward. 7

Chapter 1: January 24, 2010 11

Chapter 2: Confusion and Disbelief 19

Chapter 3: Twins. 25

Chapter 4: School. 31

Chapter 5: The Younger Years. 35

Chapter 6: Life As A Teenager. 39

Chapter 7: Full of Life. 47

Chapter 8: Graduation. 55

Chapter 9: Friends Memories. 61

Chapter 10: KDR Challenge Journey. 79

Chapter 11: Kelsey's Law. .89

Chapter 12: The Signing. 97

Chapter 13: Questioning God. 103

Chapter 14: In Her Own Words 111

Chapter 15: Signs from God 131

Chapter 16: Moving On Without Kelsey. 137

Kelsey Dawn Raffaele

Chapter 1:
January 24, 2010

3:37 p.m.

My cell phone rang.

"Hello?"

"Bonnie, this is Stacey. Kelsey has been in an accident."

"Where are you?"

"Down by the high school... It is really bad Bonnie."

"Did she roll the car?"

"No."

"We are on our way."

It was freezing rain on that Sunday. The roads were slippery in spots and slushy in other areas. I remember thinking on our way to Kelsey that everything was going to be okay. My goodness, they were down by the high school and she didn't roll the car. At that time, I thought Stacey had been in the car with Kelsey. If Stacey was talking to me, Kelsey probably broke her leg or something. As we turned onto Seymour Street, I saw all the emergency vehicles further down the road.

It was then that my heart sank to the pit of my stomach and I realized this wasn't good. I kept telling Ronnie to drive faster and he kept telling me he couldn't go any faster. It felt like an eternity before we got to the scene. I jumped out of our vehicle before it had even come to a complete stop. An officer was standing in front of his car. I saw an ambulance, fire truck, state police, city police and sheriff cars.

I screamed at the officer that my daughter was in the car. The look on his face was pure horror. I was able to get around him and what I saw will forever be embedded in my mind. In the crumpled up car, there was no passenger seat anymore. I saw my baby slumped over and not moving. I saw her long blonde hair.

I screamed for her. "Kelsey! Oh my God, no! Not Kelsey." I tried to get to her, but the police officer wouldn't let me go.

He said, "You don't want to make her upset."

I looked at him and said, "She isn't moving, I want to go to her."

But he wouldn't let me go.

Ronnie was behind me, kneeling on the cold pavement crying. Then Stacey was there crying and a gentleman was holding her up. I didn't recognize the man.

I looked at Stacey and said, "Is she breathing?"

Stacey just stared at me.

"There is a heartbeat," the gentleman answered.

I knew by the way he said it, she wasn't going to make it. I knew she was slipping away right there. I could feel it.

The police officer suggested we head to the hospital. They didn't want us driving so an officer was instructed to drive us.

> *It was then that my heart sank to the pit of my stomach and I realized this wasn't good.*

I asked again if I could go with my baby, and they said "No." Yet another sign that it wasn't good.

We got into the police car and headed to the hospital. On the way I called my sister Lori. All I got out was, "Lori, Kelsey has been in an accident." I didn't even tell her how bad it was before she said she was on her way.

I called my other sister, Debbie, next and told her that Kelsey was in an accident and she needed to go to my house, and get Courtney, Kelsey's twin sister, and bring her to the hospital.

We made it to the hospital before the ambulance arrived. They took us into a room where Ronnie and I were all alone. He was crying so hard that he was getting sick. I remember telling him that everything was going to be okay when I knew it wasn't. My years of working in the medical field, told me this wasn't going to have a good outcome. But I tried to be the strong one.

Lori arrived a few minutes later. I told her we had to have someone go and get Mom and Dad. Lori called her son, Joshua, and told him what was going on and to get Grandma and Grandpa. She said to not tell them what had happened until they were close to the hospital. A few minutes later, Debbie came with Courtney.

Courtney looked at me and said, "What happened?"

I told Courtney that it didn't look good and we needed to be prepared for the worse. She, being the strong girl that she is, went into "I'll take care of everyone mode."

About an hour or so later, a nurse came in and gave us a quick update. She informed us that Kelsey did have a heartbeat but they had to put a breathing tube in her because her lungs had collapsed.

The emergency room waiting area was filled with family and friends so they moved us to another room. I called Ronnie's mom and told her she needed to come.

Sometime later the ER doctor gave us an update. The right side of her jaw was smashed and she had a severe head injury. Her ribs were broken and she couldn't breathe on her own. Her pelvis was broken in several places. She basically had been crushed by the passenger side of the car. He told us he was trying to stabilize her so they could transport her to a trauma center.

His exact words were, "She is gravely ill... It doesn't look good and we need to prepare for the worst."

By this time, more people had gathered at the hospital. There were well over a hundred of Kelsey's friends sitting in the halls of the hospital. I went out, thanked them all for coming and said things weren't looking too good so could they please pray for a miracle.

We were able to go in and see Kelsey. Ronnie and I went in first. We were in shock. I couldn't believe this was happening to our family. I stepped into the room and there lying on the stretcher was my baby. She had tubes coming out of her from all over. I went to hold her hand and I let go as soon as I touched it. I knew that feeling from working in the hospital – it was the feeling of death.

I went up to her and started "petting her like a dog" (she always asked me to do that). I leaned into her ear and whispered that I loved her and Mommy was there. I remember someone standing by her head wiping away the blood and I kept saying, "She is bleeding too much." As I walked out of her room, the surgeon — that we knew well — was there and I asked him to please save her. He just looked at me and said he was going to do his best.

Ronnie, Courtney, and I huddled on the floor in the waiting area.

My sweet Courtney kept saying, "We will get through this."

> *My sweet Courtney kept saying, "We will get through this."*

She looked at Ronnie and I and said, "Let's promise this won't break our family apart. We have to stay strong for each other." We promised we would make it through this together as a family.

Three and a half hours after the call from Stacey, the surgeon came out of the operating room with tears in his eyes. "Bonnie, I did everything I could. I couldn't save her." he said.

I asked to see her again.

Ronnie and I walked in to see our baby for the last time. I felt like I was in a dream. Still not believing this was happening to me; to our family. How could God give me these two beautiful children and then take one away so soon? It's not supposed to be this way. I kissed my baby on the head and told her again how much I loved her. Then I turned and walked out the door.

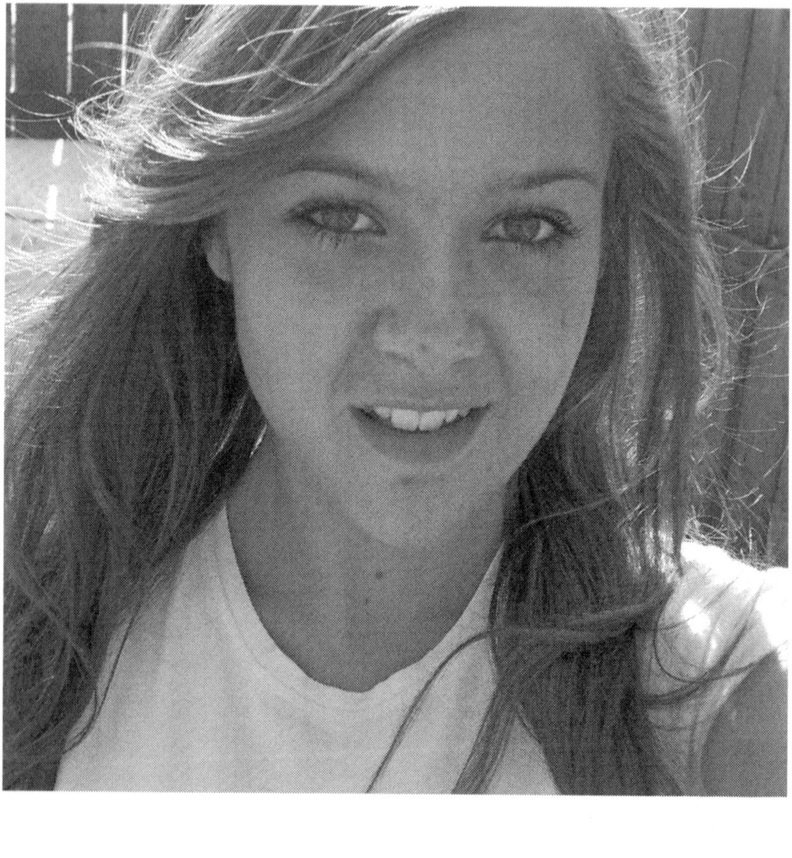

Chapter 2: Confusion and Disbelief

As we arrived home, the phone was ringing. I answered it. It was Kelsey's friend, Eric. He was in the Army and stationed in South Korea. He was crying.

"Bonnie, please tell me it isn't true," Eric asked.

"I'm so sorry Eric, it is true. She is gone," I said. I still wasn't crying. We were all in shock.

We always thought Kelsey would end up marrying Eric. He had just been home for Christmas and asked if Kelsey could come to South Korea after she graduated.

I had told him, "You can have her when you get stationed in Hawaii, but she's not going to Korea." We all got a laugh out of it.

After I hung up with Eric, the phone rang again. It was Ben, another of Kelsey's friends. He too was begging me to tell him it wasn't true.

The phone kept ringing, and ringing, and ringing that night — mostly Kelsey's friends.

I still wasn't crying; I had to take care of the kids. I had to show them that Kelsey was okay. She was in Heaven with God and she was okay.

> *I had to take care of the kids...*
> *...to show them that Kelsey was okay.*

We didn't sleep much that night. I was up throughout the night, just sitting on the sofa. The next morning one of my good friends was at my door with food. He had lost his daughter years earlier and knew what we were going through.

Later that morning we had to go to the funeral home to make arrangements for Kelsey's funeral. (I still have a hard time saying that.) I can't explain how hard it was to plan her funeral. This wasn't right. I shouldn't be planning my daughter's funeral. I worked so hard to have a baby, I shouldn't be doing this. It just wasn't fair.

Much of it was a blur. I remember flipping through a book of caskets and Ronnie and I pointed to a casket at the same time. We knew that was the one for her. Writing up her obituary, deciding where we were going to bury her, and who was going to do the service - all of this is a blur.

The next few days were the worst. The wake and funeral

was one of the largest in town. Over one thousand people attended. I chuckle as I type that. Kelsey would hang out with Ronnie and me on a lot of weekends and watched movies together. I would always ask her, why she wasn't out with her friends. She would always tell us that she didn't have any friends. I cannot wait to get to Heaven and scold her for saying that. I met all her friends – all one thousand of them.

Ronnie and I stood by Kelsey's casket the entire time. I remember my friends trying to get me to sit down, but I told them I had to take care of the kids. I needed to tell them that Kelsey was in Heaven and they needed to be saved so they could see her again. They were all so upset. I had to take care of them. Kelsey would have wanted me to help them.

The outpouring of love and support came from not just family and friends, but our entire community. You know people ask me why I stayed in the Sault (our hometown) after I graduated from high school. I would always say, "I had a blonde moment." But after receiving so much support from the community, I would never want to be anywhere else.

The cards were unbelievable. We received hundreds of them. I still have every one of them. The money that was sent to us was unbelievable. Ronnie and I decided to create a scholarship at Lake Superior State University in Kelsey's name. Within a few months of her death this scholarship had received enough money to be endowed. It will always be there for a student from Sault High School.

As the days went by, I found out more about the accident. I needed to know what happened to my baby. Was she afraid? Did she call out for me? I had to know. So the story goes....

Kelsey and her best-friend, Stacey, who was driving her own car, were on their way to our house to drop off Kelsey's car. Kelsey wanted a Coke Freezy from Walmart. Stacey was following her. They were on Seymour Street which is by the high school. There was a slower moving vehicle ahead of her, so Kelsey switched lanes to pass it. Stacey went out to pass, but realized she didn't have enough time to get by and got back in behind the slower vehicle. It was at that point, Stacey knew Kelsey was in trouble and prayed that she would make it past. Kelsey was able to pass the car, but clipped the snow bank when she got back in her lane and overcorrected turning out into the path of the oncoming vehicle. The oncoming vehicle was only traveling at 35 miles-per-hour when it T-boned Kelsey.

A couple days after the accident I found out Kelsey was talking on her phone when she went out to pass the car. We had heard how dangerous texting and driving was and the girls were told to never text and drive. I did not know how dangerous talking and driving was as well. Kelsey was so into the conversation on the phone that she wasn't paying attention to driving.

I spoke to the person she was on the phone with and my daughters last words were, "Oh shit, I'm going to crash." Kelsey knew she was in trouble. She knew she had made a mistake.

The person she was talking to said the phone went dead after she said that and he tried to call her back but there was no answer. The phone was found in her back seat. We believe that once Kelsey went out to pass, she realized she was in trouble. She hung up the phone and tossed it into the back seat and then put both hands on the wheel to try and pass the car safely.

I also spoke to the person she had passed that day. He and I graduated from high school together. I asked him if he thought Kelsey was afraid. He said that everything happened so fast, he estimated six seconds from the time she went out to pass to the time she was hit, that she didn't have enough time to really be afraid. He believes that it was quick.

Courtney and Kelsey

Chapter 3: Twins

All I ever wanted to be in life was a mom. Because of some medical reasons; we weren't sure I was ever going to be able to have children. After years of trying, I found out I was pregnant. We were so excited. Early on in the pregnancy I became very sick; I lost almost 10 pounds in the first couple of months. My doctor decided we needed to see what was going on so he ordered an ultrasound. To our delight, we found out that I was not having one baby, but two. What a blessing! After trying for so long, God blessed me with two babies.

I went to my parents' house to tell them the great news. My dad was working, so I called him.

"Daddy, guess what?" I said.

He said "What?"

"I'm having twins," I said.

Silence on the phone.

"Daddy, did you hear me? Are you surprised?" I said.

"Nothing you do surprises me, Bonnie," Dad said with a chuckle.

It was a rough few months, but I loved being pregnant. At 26 weeks I went into labor. I went to a hospital in Petoskey, Michigan where the doctors fought to stop my labor and to save my babies. I was never worried about them, I knew God gave me this blessing and everything was going to be fine. Ronnie and everyone else prayed that God would take care of them and everything would be fine.

> *All I ever wanted to be in life was a mom....*

After six weeks in the hospital, I was able to go home, but was on strict bed rest.

I remember those days like it was yesterday. I was so bored, but knew I had to do what the doctors told me to do in order to keep the babies safe. So I watched TV, cross-stitched, did word puzzles, rubbed lotion on my belly and talked to the babies.

At week thirty-two, I once again was in labor. I was shipped back to Petoskey where the doctors did tests and determined that the babies were big enough to be born.

On May 2, 1992 at 2:23 a.m., I was blessed with a

daughter, Courtney Sue. She was tiny, only 3lbs, 4oz, but she was healthy and screaming at the top of her lungs. At 2:30 a.m., I was blessed once again with another daughter, Kelsey Dawn. She was a little bigger than Courtney, weighing 4lbs, 4oz., but she too was healthy. God had blessed me with not one, but two healthy children. My miracle babies.

Courtney Sue was named after her grandpa, my dad. His middle name is Courtney. Kelsey Dawn was named after a friend of Ronnie and mine, Leslie Dawn, who was killed in an automobile accident while I was pregnant with the girls.

It was the best thing ever. I loved being a mom, watching them grow and seeing the expressions on their faces as they learned new things; watching them learn to crawl and walk and talk; seeing how much fun they had playing together, how they watched out for each other, and how they were best friends.

Kelsey seemed to always take care of Courtney. I have a video of Kelsey feeding Courtney her breakfast when they were two. Courtney had an ear to ear smile as her sister fed her. You can hear me in the video telling Courtney to feed her sister. She wouldn't have anything to do with that. She was content with Kelsey taking care of her.

I remember when they were in preschool the teacher told us that they needed to separate the girls into different groups. All I could say was, "Good luck with that". One teacher took Courtney to the water table in the classroom and the other teacher took Kelsey to the drawing table in the classroom. Kelsey wasn't happy when the teacher told her that she wasn't going to be with her sister that day. The little fire cracker that she was, looked up at the teacher and said, "I want my sister and I want her now." She didn't get her sister and they were in separate groups the rest of the school year.

You hear stories of twins that talk to each other in their own language, or them sensing when something is wrong with the other one. I am here to tell you that it is all true.

Kelsey

One day while the girls were in preschool, they were sitting at different tables. The teachers instructed the class to draw a picture of themselves. Courtney drew a picture of her and Kelsey, and Kelsey, sitting across the room did the same. I still have those pictures. They would also carry on a conversation in a language only they knew. It was amazing watching them answer each other and I didn't understand a word they were saying.

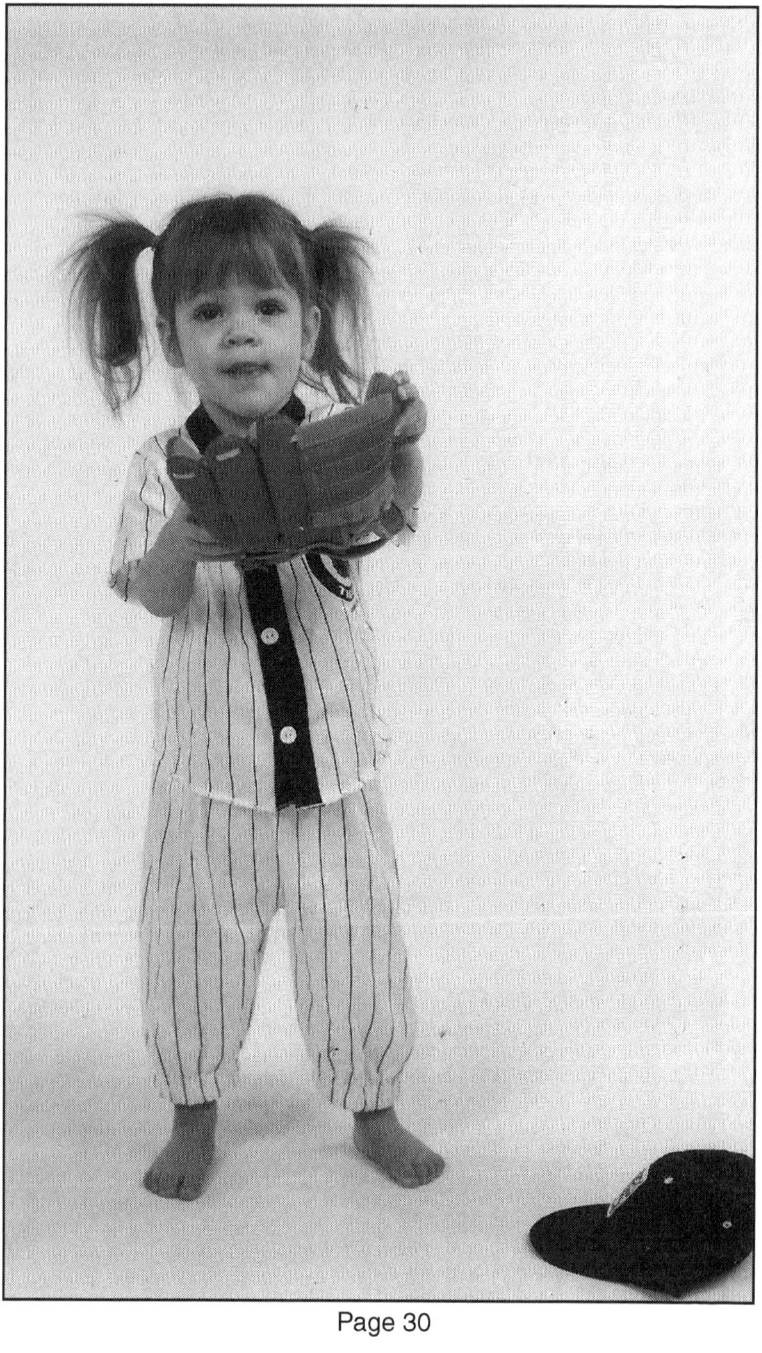

Chapter 4: School

First day of kindergarten was an experience. The girls were so shy. I remember at kindergarten roundup, Courtney would not say a single word. All she would do was sit on my lap and stare at the lady that was asking her questions. I was so afraid they were going to tell me the girls weren't ready for kindergarten. But they didn't. I was happy, but sad. My little girls were growing up.

I took them to school on the first day. I walked them to their room and I could tell they were scared. They sat down in chairs, but as I turned to leave, both girls got up from their chairs, ran across the room and wrapped themselves around my legs crying. I held back my tears as the teacher came and took them. I went across the road to my sister's house where I could see the playground and their kindergarten room. I stood there the whole time they were there, (half-days back then), and looked out the window wondering what they were doing and wondering if they were okay.

They came out for recess and I saw them look over at

Aunt Lori's. I was back some from the window so they couldn't see me. Courtney was a little more timid then Kelsey was. I could see Kelsey had already made friends and was playing on the playground with them. Courtney went straight to the swings. She sat in one of them facing Aunt Lori's house and swung the entire time. She was so fixated on looking at her aunt's house that she missed the whistle to go in. She just sat there swinging. The teacher didn't realize she forgot a child so Aunt Lori went out and told Courtney to go inside. Poor little Courtney had to bang on the classroom window for someone to let her in. Of course she was crying, but she was brave and went back into class.

> *I was fortunate to be able to work in school system. This allowed me to have the summers off and be with the girls.*

I was fortunate to be able to work in the school system. This allowed me to have the summers off and be with the girls. We did so many things together. We would have picnics in the back yard, they would swim in the pool or play on the swing set. I would take them to the park and to see their dad at work.

Some days during the summer I would have to go into work and the girls LOVED going to Mommy's office and play. They would take my chair (it had wheels) and push each other up and down the hall at the school.

I was the cheerleading coach for Brimley Schools. The girls would go to the games with me and cheer. They thought they were pretty cool having their own cheerleading outfit and hanging out with the older cheerleaders. Of course everyone thought they were the cutest thing ever.

The girls were so close that I decided that when they entered school we would not split them up. The girls were in the third grade and had the same teacher they had as when they were in the first grade. During one of the last parent-teacher conferences that year the teacher told us that she was seeing a difference in Kelsey. She wasn't as confident as she had been in the first grade and her grades were not as good. She recommended we separate the girls for the fourth grade. I originally said no but after thinking about it we decided to do it. So for the rest of their elementary years, the girls were in separate classes. It wasn't until years later that Courtney and Kelsey told me that Kelsey cried all the time because she wanted to be in the same class as Courtney. If I had known that, I would have put them back together.

And we know that God causes all things to work together for good to those who love God, to those who are called according to His purpose.

Romans 8:28 (NASB)

Chapter 5:
The Younger Years

Throughout the years we were able to take several vacations to Florida. Ronnie's mom lived there in the winter time so we would go there during spring break. The girls were so good. On all the trips we made there, they never would be cranky in the car. The first day would be a very long day. We would drive until we were by Atlanta, stop for the night, and then get up early the next morning and finish the drive.

> *I couldn't believe my little girls would even think about eating a worm. . . .*

One year, the girls had to have been around seven, we were on our way to Florida. Ronnie was chewing gum and decided to toss it out the window. Apparently, Kelsey had

Courtney and Kelsey

gum as well and once she saw her dad toss his gum out, she rolled down her window and tossed her gum out. Courtney asked her why she did that, to which Kelsey replied, "I didn't want dad's gum to be lonely." I didn't learn about this until after Kelsey passed away. But, it didn't surprise me. That is what Kelsey was like. She had a heart of gold. She cared about everyone and everything.

It is funny the stories that come out when your children get older. Like the worm story. We were all hanging out one day talking about 'things' and this worm story came up. Apparently the girls thought that since they were twins they had to do something that would 'bond' them for life. They thought about cutting their fingers and smearing the blood together, but decided that wasn't too cool. So Courtney, yes little innocent Courtney, picked up a worm and said they should eat it. Of course Kelsey agreed. So, Courtney took the worm, ripped it in half and gave one half to Kelsey. Together, they put the worm in their mouths and swallowed it. Yep, they ate the worm. I about died laughing when they told the story. I couldn't believe my little girls would even think about eating a worm let alone actually doing it.

But they did.

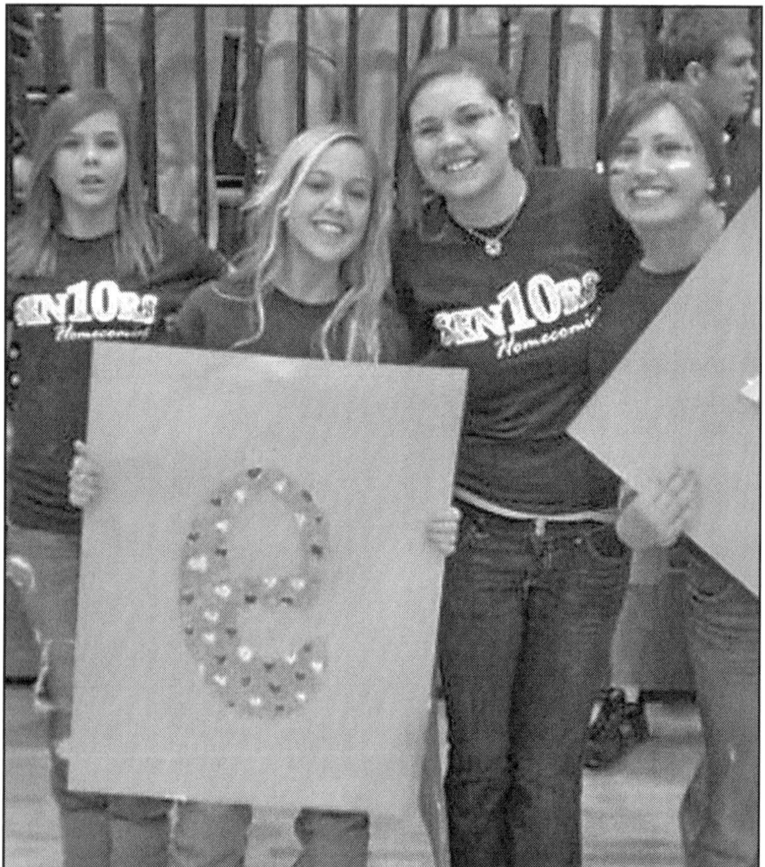

Chapter 6: Life as a Teenager

Junior High was a trying time for the girls, especially for Kelsey. I believe it is the hardest years for kids these days. They are not children anymore, but not yet adults. There are so many things they need to figure out.

Seventh grade was the hardest for Kelsey. She wanted everyone to like her and got in with the wrong crowd. I was working at the school district so I was able to keep an eye on her and Courtney. We had a rule in our house that the girls could not wear makeup at that age. One day, I just happened to be in the junior high working on some computer issues. The bell rang for classes to change. I look down the hall and here comes Kelsey with all this makeup on her face. She looked up and saw me and by the look on her face I knew she was scared. I calmly took her into one of the classrooms and told her to go straight to the bathroom and wash the makeup off her face. She did.

Later on that night, at home, I asked Kelsey if she understood why I didn't approve of her wearing so much makeup. She said she didn't understand. I told her that the way she looked boys would think that she wasn't a "good girl." She started crying and said, "Mom, I am not like that. I would never do anything bad." I told her I knew that and she knew that, but the kids at school, especially the boys, would think differently. She never wore makeup like that again.

It was lessons like that, that Kelsey learned throughout seventh and eighth grade.

Then came high school. Both girls tried out for the Pom Pon squad when they were freshman. Courtney made the team, but Kelsey didn't. This devastated Courtney. You would think that Kelsey would be the one sad, but it was her sister. That evening Courtney was sitting on the couch crying, saying she didn't want to be on the team without Kelsey. Kelsey came in from outside and said, "Courtney, I'm not sad I didn't make it. Don't cry. You stay on the squad. I'm okay." My eyes filled with tears. I was so proud of both of them. Courtney stayed on the squad and had a great time.

Sophomore year, Courtney tried out again for Poms. I begged Kelsey to, but she kept telling me no. So I did what any good mother would do, I bribed her. I told her that if she tried out I would give her one hundred dollars. Yes, I was desperate. So, she tried out and made the squad. That year she was quoted in the yearbook after being asked why she tried out for poms, as saying, "My mom paid me one hundred dollars to try out." Yes, everyone in Sault Sainte

Marie knew I bribed my child. Looking back it is funny.

Courtney continued to be a Pom girl all four years of high school. She became captain for her junior and senior year. Courtney also made the All-Star squad at summer camp 2009. Kelsey and I took some of the girls to camp that year. We made a "mini vacation" out of it. Mom and Daughter time. We went to Traverse City, MI to see one of my friends and would travel back to camp to see Courtney perform. It was a fun time for us. I am so glad we did it as it

> *Yes, everyone in Sault Sainte Marie knew I bribed my child. Looking back it is funny.*

was the last summer Kelsey was alive. I look back on that time as a blessing. Just Kel and I hanging out. Oh what I would give to be able to just hang out with her one more time.

Kelsey was on the squad for just her sophomore and junior years. She wanted to enjoy her last year of high school and, she said there was too much "drama" on the squad. It's funny, she wasn't on the squad her senior year, but she would get up at 7 a.m. that summer and go to practice with Courtney. I kept asking her why she didn't try out. It didn't make any sense to me that she would be getting up and going to practice and not want to be on the squad. I guess this way, she wasn't in the "Drama" and if she didn't want to get up she didn't have to.

Every year there would be a Pom banquette at the end of the season. It would be dinner in the high school library and the coach would give out certificates and talk about each of the girls. Kelsey's last year on the squad was her junior year. She was crying when the coach was talking about her. Sometimes I wonder if she really wanted to quit.

> *Kelsey fought for having an "In Loving Memory" page in the year book for Brett. . . .*

After the certificates were handed out it was picture time. We always took pictures of the squad and of course Courtney and Kelsey. That year, Kelsey and Courtney had something up their sleeve. They asked me to wait as they turned their backs to me. When they came back around Courtney had glasses on that had a mustache on them. Kelsey turned and kissed Courtney on the cheek. As you can see by the picture, it turned out to be an adorable picture of them. Kelsey was always hugging on Courtney. She took care of her sister all the time.

2007 was a tough year for Kelsey. In February, Brett, her "boyfriend" from the fifth grade, died of cancer. She took this so hard. Then in July, another good friend, Chucky,

Courtney and Kelsey

died in a swimming accident. Kelsey was beside herself. She decided she was going to do anything and everything she could do to keep their memory alive. That she did. She and a few friends organized a benefit dance for Brett's mom raising over six hundred dollars for her. She made bead bracelets with the boys names on them and gave them to everyone she could. She walked in the Relay for Life every year in honor of Brett. Ronnie and I told Kelsey that she would see Brett and Chucky again in Heaven, she just had to believe in the Lord and to be good. I never really knew how this time in her life really affected her until years later.

Kelsey and Courtney were on the yearbook staff their senior year. Brett, who had passed away three years earlier, would have graduated with the girls. Kelsey fought for having an "In Loving Memory" page in the year book for Brett. It had been three years since his death and she was still making people remember him. She promised him she would keep his memory alive. She worked hard on that page.

Ironicly, we now wear beaded bracelets with Kelsey's name on it. I even wear one with Brett's name, that Kelsey had made me before she passed away. That yearbook spread for Brett a couple pages later in the yearbook, is a two page spread of Kelsey. She didn't get to see Brett's finished page.

Kelsey wrote about Brett for her Psychology class paper. It was the last paper she wrote before she passed away. In part it reads:

The most emotional time of my life would have to be the day Brett had passed away, it was also one of the worst days I've ever had. It was probably the hardest thing I have ever been through as a teenager. Just writing about him gets me worked up at times. After he had passed I had a big turn in my life and started to go down the wrong road. I wasn't really sure how to deal with the loss of a best friend. Along with three other tragic deaths followed that summer, Brett was the closest. I didn't understand why he had to go so fast. I told myself over and over again for days he wasn't really gone and that I could go to his house and he'd be there playing video games. It had finally hit me when I attended his wake. I never imagined he would actually be gone. As I was just a kid when he was first diagnosed with cancer the doctors had said he had a few months left to live, he started getting treatment and ended up living longer than what they had expected. With that being said I thought it was just another chance, that he would out live this like he had done before. I don't really want to get into my whole life story on the crazy and rough situations I had experienced after his death because that may take up a lot of time. Long story short I finally kicked it into gear and realized the things I had been doing wasn't making anything better, it was only making things worse. The pain was still there. I grew up and got some sense knocked into me. Now, I'm doing a lot better and have switched roads. I talk to Brett everyday still, to keep in touch. Even though people say I am crazy I know he can hear me. He will always be a part of me and I am looking forward to meeting him on the other side when it is my time.

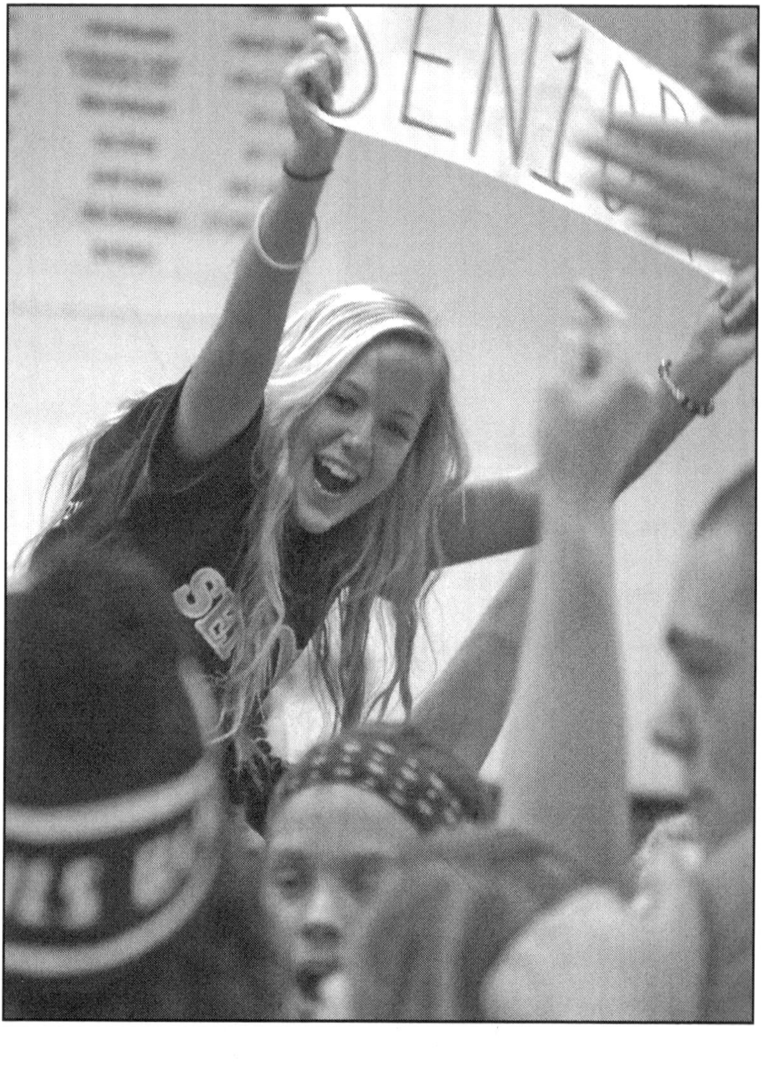

Chapter 7:
Full of Life

Kelsey was so excited for her senior year. She didn't like school much, but couldn't wait until she was a senior. She was so involved in all the activities during Homecoming week. She helped decorate the lobby and came up with the class saying, "God is Great, Life is Good, & Seniors are Crazy". I was so proud of her for coming up with it. Some of the last photos I took of her were at the homecoming pep assembly. She was one of the seniors leading the senior class into the gym. She was so, so happy. So full of life as you can see by this picture. This is one of my favorite pictures of her. The smile on her face and the excitement in her eyes is how I like to remember her.

Courtney was on homecoming court. Kelsey was so proud of her. She put signs up asking everyone to vote for Courtney. It was cold on homecoming night and it rained. Poor Courtney's feet were so cold by the end of the game that her dad had to carry her into the house. We turned the fireplace on so she could warm her feet before she went to the dance. She didn't win homecoming queen, but she had a great time at the dance.

Kelsey was in BPA, Business Professionals of America, throughout her high school years. There was regional competition in Escanaba every year. If you placed there, you moved on to state competition in Grand Rapids, Michigan. I was able to go with Kelsey all four years to Escanaba as I gave the technical tests to the students competing in that area. This was Kelsey's and my special time. We had so much fun on the trips. We went shopping, hung out at the motel, and I was able to be there to encourage her and calm her down before she competed. She placed three years out of the four she attended. I remember her senior year. I think she had the best time that year. She would help calm the new kids down before they competed and they all looked up to her. That's one thing Kelsey loved to do. She loved to help people. She always saw the good in a person even if no one else saw it. I remember on the bus ride up there I was sitting in the front and she was at the back of the bus. I texted her and asked her to come see me. I asked her to fix my hair for me as it was bugging me. She did. I can still see this in my mind. Most teenage girls wouldn't want anything to do with their mom but not my Kelsey.

Like I said, we always went shopping the day we arrived in Escanaba. I always let Kelsey go and be with her friends and I walked around. Her last year, I was walking around and I receive a text from Kel. She asked me to come to Claire's. I did and there she was with this goofy stuffed animal that played happy birthday. She had this huge smile on her face and she said, "Should I get this for Dad?" I said "Yea." She couldn't wait to get home to give her dad, her BFF, his present. We still have that stuffed animal in our room. I know he will cherish it forever.

Kelsey placed second in HTML programing that year. She was so excited she was going to States. When we got home, we made plans for all of us, including Ronnie and

Courtney, to go to the competition. Kelsey wanted to show her dad and sister what she did. She was so proud of herself. I made hotel reservations for that week. At states, they have a dance on Saturday night and Kelsey was going to take Courtney to the dance. But we didn't get to go. why?

> *This was Kelsey's and my special time....*

The girls came to me one day and asked me if I would take their senior pictures. I told them I would but they couldn't argue with me, they had to do what I asked them to do. Courtney's boyfriend, Mike, also wanted me to take his senior pictures. They were really good about it. The first place we went to was to a beach where we had taken the girls for several years when they were young. I must have taken over five hundred pictures in that spot alone. We were packing up to leave and Kelsey asked us if we had ever been to the rock quarry. We said no. She said it was a good place to take pictures. So we had her show us the way there. It was this lake in the middle of nowhere with huge rocks all around it. It was a great place to take pictures. I asked her later on that summer how she knew where this place was. She said that she and her friends had gone there a couple times. By this time, Courtney had had enough with the picture taking. Not Kelsey though. She LOVED to have her picture taken. So, I continued to snap pictures of her.

One of my favorite senior pictures was taken there. I had her sit on this huge rock. You can see in the picture the beaded bracelet with Brett's name on it — the one she wore

all the time in his honor. I now wear one in honor of her on my right wrist and I wear the one she made me in honor of Brett on my left.

A few days later I took more pictures, this time in our

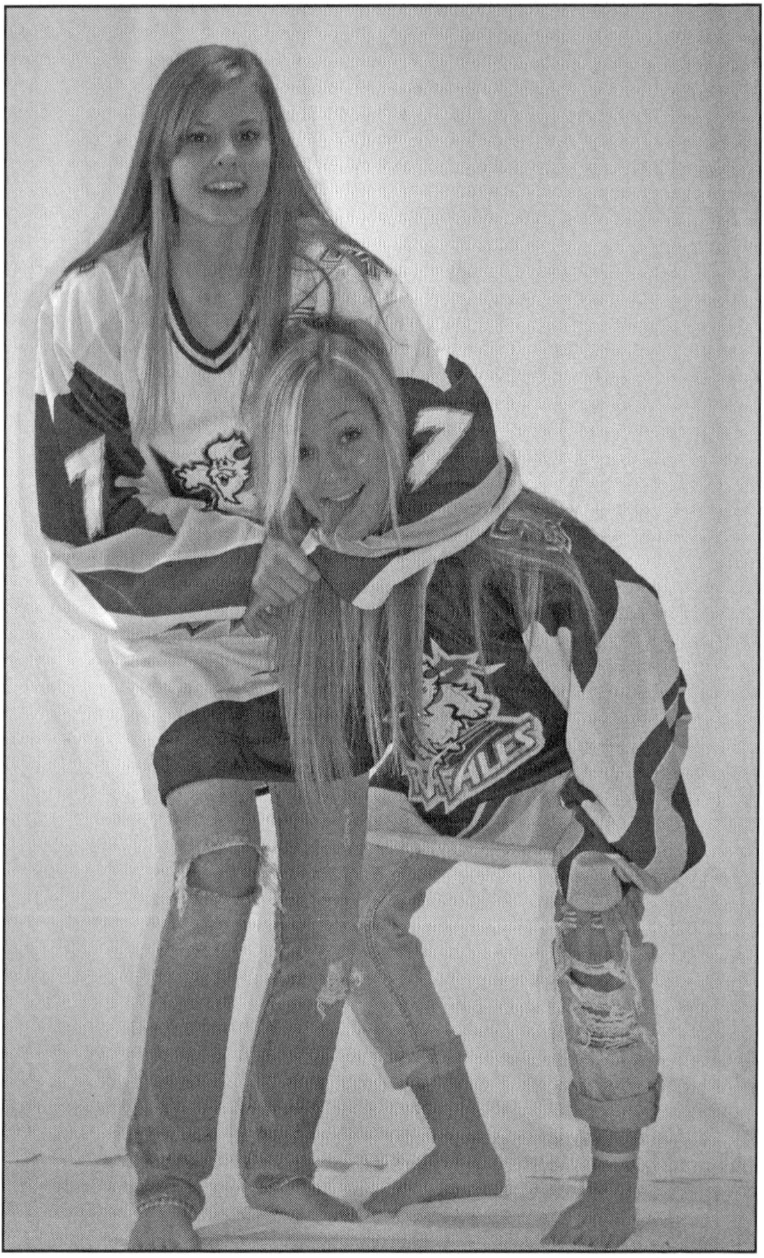
ALES

backyard. Once again I took more of Kelsey than Courtney. You have to understand, I'm not a professional photographer by any means. So it was hilarious when Kel and I were trying to get her picture in the hammock. I don't recommend taking photos outside when the wind is blowing. The results were hilarious. Kelsey's long beautiful hair was blowing all over and the hammock wouldn't stay still for her to get on. We laughed so hard that day.

The last place I wanted to take pictures was in the house. I wanted a nice picture of them together. I took over eight hundred in the house. Note to self, don't take so many pictures. It is way too hard to pick just one good one. Once again we had a blast doing it. Earlier that summer we had purchased a turtle, Skeeter, for Courtney. Of course she wanted her picture taken with it. I held the shutter down as Skeeter ran away from Courtney. This series of pictures are way too funny to look at. The expression on Courtney's face is priceless.

I have to say that this picture of the girls together is my favorite. Ronnie and I have these hockey jerseys that have "Raffaele" on the back and the name of the hockey team is "Rafales." Kelsey knew we had the jerseys and came up with the idea of using them. Love, Love, Love this picture.

All in all, we had fun taking their senior pictures. And with what has happened since then, spending so much time with the girls that summer has more meaning now than ever. Her last summer with us. The summer of 2009.

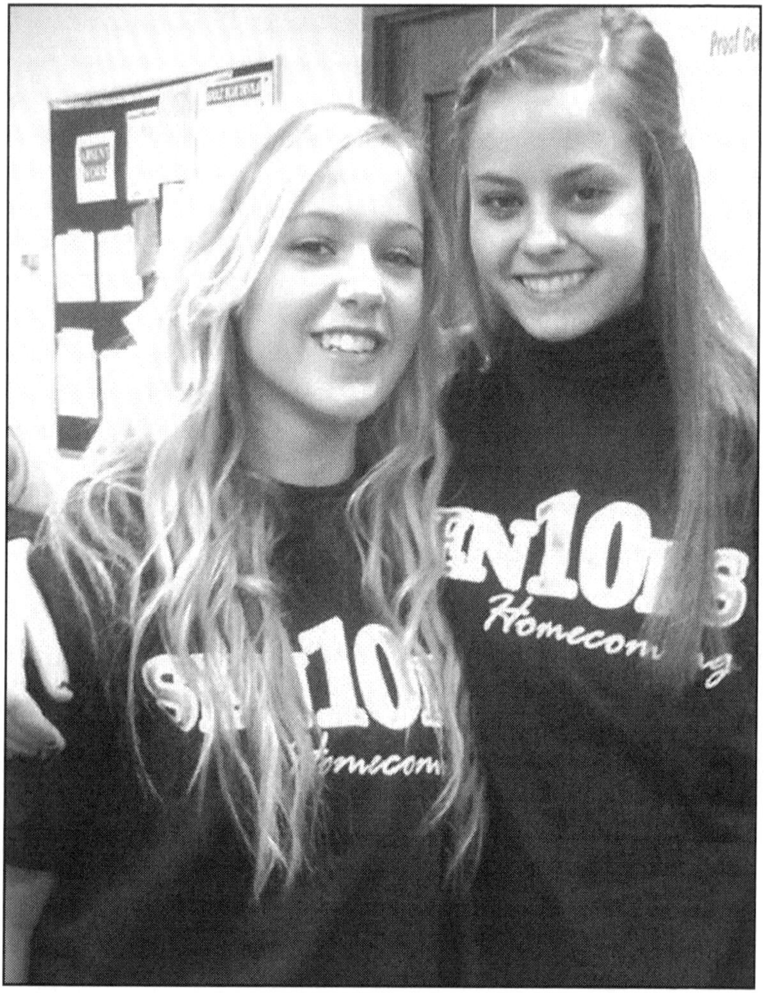

Chapter 8: Graduation

Graduation was one of the hardest days. My heart was breaking so hard for Courtney. Courtney and Kelsey were so excited to graduate, to walk across that stage together. But that didn't happen. The school and her senior class decided they wanted a chair at graduation for Kelsey. So Courtney decorated Kelsey's cap and placed it on that chair along with some flowers. Courtney wore both her tassel and Kelsey's tassel on her cap. She wore Kelsey's gown and her BPA cords. Kelsey didn't even know she was getting BPA cords. She would have been so happy. Courtney's boyfriend Mike, wore Kelsey's SAHS medal around his neck. So you see, every part of Kelsey was there that day.

One of her classmates gave a speech about Kelsey and it is as follows.

- Favorite color. Green and Black

- Favorite singer: Gwen Stefanie

- Favorite TV show: The girls next door, Kendra, and The Hills

- Favorite food: pretty much anything

- Favorite way to spend the afternoon: tanning, bleaching hair, and bleaching teeth

- Favorite animal: dog BamBam, also known as, BAMF

- Favorite Class: 2010

- Favorite hockey player: Pat Kane

- Least favorite hockey player: Sidney Crosby

- Favorite thing to do at home: text, Facebook, and pick on dad

- Favorite vacation spot: Cadillac to visit cousin Brock

- Favorite school related activity: Business Professionals of America

- Favorite way to spend free time: with friends

I'm sure you've figured out by now that I'm reading some of Kelsey Raffaele's favorite things.

I'm sure after listening to this list, you've noticed that you may have had one, two, or many things in common with Kelsey.

Also, you may have funny stories from when you were a kid, like Kelsey did. One time, when she was about three years old, Kelsey dressed up like Snow White and sang "I'm Wishing" into the toilet.

Kelsey's chair was left empty in rememberance of her.

I know that we've all done things our parents didn't know about. Kelsey pierced her belly button but her parents had no idea.

And many of us had personal experiences with Kelsey, at BPA, a Pom performance, or a hockey game.

Friends are hard to find and impossible to forget, but the memories last a lifetime. So,thank you Kelsey for the memories.

He then presented Ronnie and I with Kelsey's diploma. It was such an emotional day for everyone, but especially my little Court. She is so strong and she stood strong that day.

> *So. thank you Kelsey for the memories....*

My favorite holiday is Christmas. Yes, I spoiled the girls every year. I didn't, and don't care if they are old and don't believe in Santa Clause, I still have a Santa present under the tree for them. Well, Courtney now. I have videotaped every Christmas so I can look back on them and see how the girls had grown. It was always a fun morning for us. The girls would wake up, not too early, and yell, "Mom, can we get up?" I can still hear them saying it as if they were right here. I would tell them "just a minute." I had to get the video camera going. I wanted their reaction to the Santa presents on video. I would get it up and running and then tell them they could come out.

Christmas of 2009 wasn't any different, except Ronnie and I were up before they crawled out of bed. Courtney finished opening her gifts before Kelsey, like always. Kelsey was eating her chocolate out of her stocking. Funny, she always complained of being fat, which she wasn't, and there she sat eating all that chocolate. It was a wonderful morning like always. Just the four of us hanging out together.

After Kelsey passed away, of course I had to go through the videos. Her last Christmas with us was the first one I watched. I could hardly make it through it. I thought I was going to have a heart attack I was crying so hard. Watching her every move, taking in every word she said, and hearing that laugh of hers. I was so happy that I had these memories. At the very end of the video Kelsey says, "Last Christmas at home." Then the camera shuts off. She had plans to get her own apartment when she graduated from high school and that is what she meant by "Last Christmas at home." But, how haunting those words are now. If she or we had only known it was actually going to be her "Last Christmas at home."

I still watch the videos and I cry through all of them. But what would I do if I didn't have them to hear her voice and watch her grow throughout the years. I thank God that I have them.

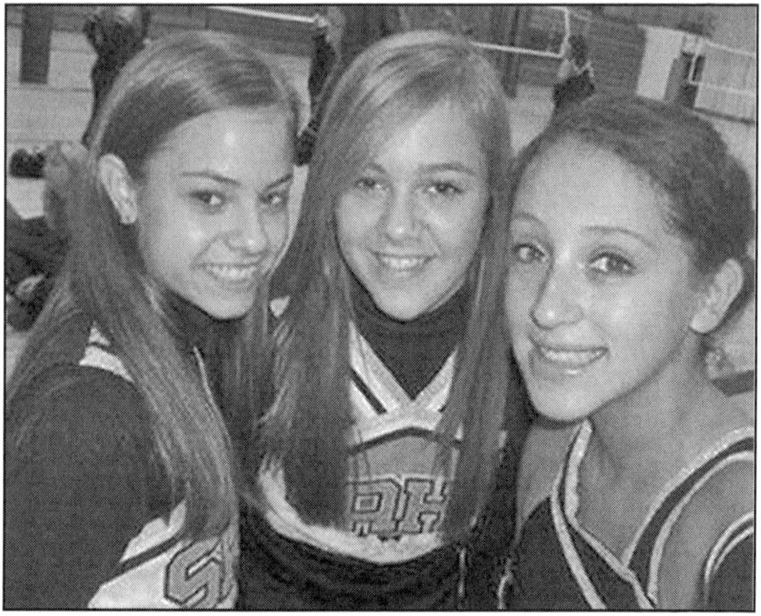

Chapter 9:
Friends' Memories

Kelsey used to stay at home a lot on weekends. Ronnie and I would always ask her why she wasn't hanging out with her friends. Her response, "I don't have any friends." We knew that wasn't true, she had lots of friends. That was proven at her wake and funeral as over one thousand friends came.

It was about a year after she passed away that I asked her friends to send me some stories as I wanted to write a book. Here are some of those stories.

Megan • *I just had a funny little memory about Kels. For our marketing Christmas party we did secret Santa's...and I was Dave's secret Santa. I was talking with Kelsey about it because I didn't know what I should get him...Kelsey immediately suggested I just tie a bow on her and give him her for Christmas. Hahaha. It reminded me of that day I saw you at the school and we were talking about how much Kelsey liked him lol....*

Megan • Here is a picture from decorating our corner for homecoming senior year. Mr. Suggitt kind of left me in charge because he was unable to be there, and nobody was really helping out. Kelsey came and stayed with me the whole day, and got a bunch of people to come out and help. Then, the junior class kept "copying" our ideas - or so we thought. Kelsey of course took matters into her own hands, and went out to make it clear to them it wasn't acceptable, haha. Then, we thought we could get them caught cheating because they were painting inside -- so Kelsey took my camera, and was sneaking around the lobby trying to catch them in the act. Lol. It was just a really fun day.

Megan • *This was just a really fun night to begin our Christmas break. For some reason, she kept calling Phil her husband. lol. And I kept protesting..saying he was mine first....then she finally got me to agree by saying "well you can just be the maid of honor" and it was kind of the joke of the night. I think her caption under this picture in her album actually was "my husband and maid of honor" lol*

Megan • *Here is another picture from the same night. It was the first night Eric got back to the Soo after being away for Bootcamp. And it was a really spur of the moment*

group. Kelsey and I were trying to figure out what to do...and didn't think much was going on. We were just watching a movie at my house, then Phil decided to come over. Then Ginny, then Jordy, then Cody, and before we knew it, Eric called and said he and Jake were on their way over. It was just a really fun night, because it wasn't planned. And it was sort of a little reunion for us. We got a lot of good pictures -- and Kelsey took it upon herself to "borrow" my camera when she went home and uploaded all my pictures herself. haha. I didn't realize til the next day, when I saw her iPod sitting in the spot my camera had been. I text her "Kelsey you left your iPod here." she said "I know, because I borrowed your camera, we can switch back later" haha.

Megan • *Summer 2009, Fourth of July weekend at Brim-*

ley State Park. Kelsey and I met up at the campground and Eric and Jake were also out there so we were all sitting around the fire. Kelsey and I went into the camper to use the bathroom or something. I was on my way back out, and Kelsey was finishing up, so I said "please turn the light off when you come out" a few minutes later, a hear big thumping noises from the camper. I opened the door to find Kelsey jumping up and down trying to reach the light to turn it off lol. I turned it off for her, and then we both just started laughing.

Megan • Kelsey and I were partners in yearbook class. We were in the ad selling group...but we never really accomplished too much. lol. After the second or third stop we'd just be done and drive around for the rest of the hour talking and trying to think of excuses of why it was taking us so long to sell the ads. Kelsey was usually better at thinking of reasons than I was. lol. That's what I remember most – driving around and talking about everything & anything. It was just a nice break at the end of the day. She'd always give me such good advice, because she'd see just about every situation differently than I did. She'd always seem to put things into perspective for me.

Jillian • I'll always remember the funniest thing when Kelsey dropped her phone in the toilet and so she yells to me Jill come stick your hand down the toilet and get my *phone, it was hilarious like i would stick my hand down there.*

Phil • *One time me, Megan, Kels, Jordy and Haley all went down to Thunder Falls in Mackinaw City. After she snuck out of the house the night before and decided to come hangout with all of us at Megan's. lol. Anyways, so we get to Thunder Falls and have a great time and go to get all of our clothes out of the lockers that you could rent from the water park. So we get our clothes and turn in the keys*

to the park and Megan realizes that she left her flip flops in one of the lockers. Megan went to go get the key back to get her flip flops but they deny her the key. Megan comes back to the car and say "well I won't be getting my shoes back, they won't give me the key." Kelsey gets out of the car and says "oh yes they will!!" Kelsey goes back inside and tells the people working the front desk that she isn't leaving until she got those flip flops back. lol. So of course we are all headed home five minutes later with sandals on all of our feet. lol.

A young man post the following on Kelsey's "In Loving Memory" Facebook page:

• Hi, this is Adam, I was in the same class with Kelsey, class of '10, and I just wanted to let you know my last moment with her, if I could? One day after school, me and my friends were sitting around outside, and she was inside practicing Pom pons. Now I never really knew her personally, but my stack of papers blew all over the place outside, and your daughter alone, who didn't even know me, came outside and helped me retrieve all of them. I just wanted to share how nice she was to not just anyone, but everyone. Thank you!!

Kelsey's friend • Okay so Kelsey always told me I look like Lindsey Lohan so when we went to the fair when I first got my license she goes "no one knows us out here so imma call you Lindsey and you call me Nicole" Nicole for Nicole

Richie cause she was blond like Kelsey. We continued calling each other that for awhile then when Jordan started hanging out with us all the time she became Paris for Paris Hilton cause she's so tall. Ironically the three of them, Lindsey, Nicole, and Paris were all best friends as well... There are so many stories I have with Kelsey but I thought I'd share this one because she loved Paris and the simple life.

Brittany B. • One time, she was driving my car and we were with Jeremy and Craig going to their house to drop them off. When all of a sudden there was all this smoke and we couldn't see anything. Kel was scared and didn't know what to do. luckily we were right in front of Jeremy's house. We pulled in and got out and there were flames coming out *of my tires! At that point we were all scared. I told kelsey to shut off my car and took her by the hand and walked away just in case. It was so cold out that night and of course I wasn't wearing my jacket. Kelsey let go of my hand and ran back to the car. I was yelling at her to get back! She opened the trunk so i walked over to her and asked her what she was doing. She said "I noticed you were cold so I came to get you my Cadillac hoodie" and handed it to me to put on. She always made sure everyone was okay before worrying about herself.*

Brittany B. • *One time Kel and I wanted to rent a movie. So the boss said she would take us to the video store. We were getting ready to leave and all of a sudden Paps goes "nothing PG or PG-13." Kel and I were so bummed because there was nothing to get now. We were talking about movies to get and the boss said we could always get "HOOK" and pretended her finger was a hook, and asked Paps if that was still to scary. Paps tried not too laugh but he couldn't help it!*

Brittany B. • *One time I was at the house (like most of my life) and it was lunch time! I'm sure Paps knows where I'm going with this! We decided that we wanted him to make us grilled cheese's. Kel and I went to play while paps made our lunch's. He called us when it was done and we sat down to eat it! It looked so delicious, but when I took that first bite I noticed something was wrong. He left the wrapper on my cheese and cooked it!!!!! We laughed and laughed until our stomach's hurt! Still to this day we joke about him making me a grilled cheese!*

Stacey • *Kelsey's senior year October 1st on Brett's birthday she wanted me to wear the Brett shirts with her. I said I would but it wasn't till the morning of the 1st that I realized I have been wearing that shirt for gym. When I got to school there was Kelsey sitting on a bench waiting for me. The first thing she noticed was I didn't have my shirt on and I told her why. Kelsey looked at me and said "I don't care if you wore it to gym the past month, little alone a few days - you're going to go get it and you're going to wear it." And I did just that.*

Stacey • *Kelsey's senior year there was a volleyball tournament for the Sault High girls in Petoskey. Mariah let us take her car. It was Kelsey, Lindsy, Mitchell, Brad, and Myself. Kelsey had just got her license and wanted to drive so we let her, she was so scared of getting pulled over or anything that she drove like 35 the whole way. We got to the game as they were handing out the trophies. When we had left the Sault we ran into another group of kids at the gas station that were going to the same game but they drove the speed limit and got there on time for the game. It was a fun little road trip filled with memories, even though we missed the game we had more fun on that car ride then we probably would of had at the game.*

Kelsey's friend • *When I was first starting Sault Area Schools in 8th grade, I was so nervous and didn't know anybody. I was feeling like it was a big mistake to transfer and was half way regretting it until Kelsey introduced her-*

self to me. I was in my 3rd hour (I believe) and Kelsey and Brittany were one of the first few people to talk to me. She just came up and started talking to me as if we'd known each other all our lives. She invited me over to sleep over after only knowing me like a week. She introduced me to her friends and showed me the ropes. After getting to know each other, we started to get really close. We spent a lot of the weekends together watching The Simple Life and listen-

ing to No Doubt. We'd sneak out to the play house at night and play games and listen to music. We'd go to the sand dunes and soak up the sun. We'd gossip till the wee hours of the morning. She was one of the most kind and welcoming souls I ever met.

Brittany S. • *I met Kelsey in kindergarten in which Tenley introduced us. After the first day we met, we were inseparable. She was so funny and such a good friend. I remember we would pass notes in class and hope not to get caught. She would come to every birthday and I remember we always told each other we would be friends no matter what. I remember we used to do talent shows and she would always let me win, and we never stopped being friends even when we hung out with different people in middle and high school. She was a beautiful person inside and out. I love and miss her everyday.*

Travis • *Well I was just talking to Brock about Kelsey, and tonight we both put KR on our sticks for her. We were just talking about how we would call her at like 3:30 in the morning and she would ALWAYS answer. And then she was gonna meet us down in St. Ignace while we were on our way home at like 7 in the morning. I'm not the type of person to just jump on the band wagon and stuff like that, and be like we were best friends and everything along those lines. We were friends, but our relationship grew while*

Brock and I were out in Hudson last year.

I just wanted to let you know, that I told Brock, every game since she left us, during our National Anthem, I say a little Prayer to Kelsey. Just telling her to take care of Brock and I during the game and to give us the strength to play well and to watch over us and keep us safe.

I know she's there and I know she takes care of Brock and I. I can feel her there at the Pullar or in Hudson or wherever we are.

> ### *He left the wrapper on my cheese and cooked it....*

Kelsey's friend • *I didn't know Kelsey very well, but I have one memory I will never forget. I would love to share this with you. Well this is how my memory goes: On September 12, 2009 my aunt passed away. But the next day after lunch I saw my aunts son. As soon as I saw him I burst into tears. I went into Mrs. Harrington's for some tissues and out of nowhere Kelsey came up to me and hugged me. She touched my heart that day and I will never forget that moment for the rest of my life. I had to share this with you* because I think of this every day and it just makes my day a little better. Thanks for letting me use some of your time to share this with you.

Kelsey's friend • Every year we hand out a scholarship in Kelsey's name to a senior planning on attending LSSU. Each student is required to write an essay on why they think they deserve the scholarship. At the time of this writing, we have handed out three awards. All students that have been awarded have deserved the award, but one essay really stands out. Here is what Jena wrote:

Inspiring Angel

Inspiration is the one word I would use to describe Kelsey Raffaele. The reason I chose this word to describe Kel is because I learned so many positive things from her. Kelsey would not only stand up for herself, but would stand up for anyone, whether she knew them or not. Kelsey was the type of friend that would be there for you no matter what, through thick and thin, despite the thoughts of others. One thing I will never forget about Kelsey was her ability to make me laugh. If I was having a bad day, Kel was always there. The most important characteristic that I learned from Kelsey is to stand up for what I believe in.

I met Kel at the end of my eighth grade year. She was the sister of my best friend and the three of us spent countless hours together. Perhaps one of the fondest memories with Kel was when we were in Chicago for poms my sophomore

year. Although Kelsey was not dancing she went to support her sister. One night after competition she came to my room to visit. We spent the majority of our night singing and dancing to the song "Thug Story" by Taylor Swift. After we settled down, Kel informed me that she had recorded a very embarrassing video of me dancing, and rapping the song. We wrestled for ten minutes, because with my reputation at stake I knew I had to delete the video. However, we agreed that she could keep the video for laughs as long as she didn't show anyone. This memory is so special to me because she later informed me that every time she was having a bad day, she would watch the video to cheer her up. Till this day it makes me feel good to know I could brighten the day of a person who was known for brightening the days of others.

Kel was one of the most outgoing people I knew. One of the funniest things I have ever seen was when Kelsey printed off hundreds of flyers with pictures of her sister and her sister's boyfriend to be voted class couple. She was running through the halls handing them out to fellow students, asking teachers to put them up on their bulletin boards, and screaming, "Courtney and Mike for class cou-

> *The most important character that I learned from Kelsey is to stand up for what I believe in....*

ple!" Embarrassed, Courtney followed Kel as best as she could to take down the flyers. Kelsey's outgoing attitude has inspired me to be a more outgoing person myself.

As I reminisce on all the memories I have with Kel, I remember all the times she would tell me about the memories she once had with Brett and Chucky, who are no longer here. It's hard to believe that I now live from memories *made with her as she once lived from memories she made with them. Not a day went by where she didn't think about the friends she had lost. Now not a day goes by where I don't think about Kelsey.*

Throughout the last two years, I have followed the most important thing that Kelsey has taught me, to stand up for what I believe in. Kelsey has truly helped me evolve into the person I am today. Her outgoing personality inspires me to try new things. Kelsey lived life to the fullest, and everything she did, she did for a reason. Not a day went by that Kelsey didn't think about the friends she had lost, and whether I get this scholarship or not, not a day will go by that I won't think about Kelsey.

ING PRIDE
THE KDR CHALLENGE
KIDS DRIVING RESPONSIBLY
KDR Challenge
I took the challenge...

Chapter 10:
KDR Challenge Journey

On the one year anniversary of her death, my friend, Ailene, who is a State Police Trooper, called me to see how I was doing. I told her that something had to be done about using your cell phones and driving, especially for the new drivers. Over the next few months, I came up with a plan to speak to high schools and tell Kelsey's story. Hopefully that would help save lives.

The KDR Challenge was created. The name of the organization came to me in the middle of the night. KDR Challenge, Kids Driving Responsibly, and KDR just so happens to be Kelsey's initials, Kelsey Dawn Raffaele. I credit the Lord for giving me the name. It couldn't be more perfect.

My first presentation was given on April 18, 2011. This just happened to be the one year anniversary of when we buried Kelsey. I was so nervous. I didn't know how the students were going to react. Were they going to listen to what I was saying? Were they going to stop using their phone's while they were driving? How was I going to know if they were listening to me? Was I going to be able to do this without crying? I was at the high school Kelsey and Courtney went to. All I could do was pray that I got through to them.

The presentation starts with having the students take out their cell phones and send a simple text to their mom. While they were doing it, we timed how long it took. It took them approximately ten seconds to send the text. I tell them that this became very important later on and they had to remember how long it took them. Next I show them a news clip of a lady texting while she was walking in a mall and she falls into the fountain. Of course the students think this is funny. The lady is interviewed and she comments that she thought she had enough distance before reaching the fountain. She thought she had enough time to send the text before reaching the fountain. I tell the students that they have to remember thats as well.

I tell them it is now time to get serious. I start off telling them about Courtney and Kelsey and how the day they were born was the happiest day of my life. I show them pictures of the girls growing up and tell them how close they were. As I am talking you could hear a pin drop. I knew I had their full attention. I continue telling them about Kelsey and how she was the caring one; how she loved to hug the ones she loved; how she took care of her sister (Courtney) and how she picked on her dad all the time. I talk about how she was just starting her life. She was getting ready to graduate from high school and move on to the next chapter of her life.

Then I talk about the day. January 24, 2010 at 3:37 p.m. I don't leave anything out and I show a picture of the car she was in. I tell them how Ronnie and I were called to the scene by Kelsey's best friend and how we could see our baby still in the car. I take them through what happened second by second. How Kelsey's last words were not "Mommy I love you" or a cry for help, but were "Oh shit, I'm going to crash." I describe what we believe happened; how once she said those words, she hung up the phone and tossed it in the back seat. How do I know that? Because that is where they found her phone. She then was able to pass the car and get back in but how she clipped the snow bank and jerked the wheel which put her into the path of the oncoming vehicle. I ask them what the lady had said about falling into the fountain. "I thought I had enough time." Just like Kelsey thought she had enough time to pass. I ask them how many seconds it took to send the text. It took Kelsey six seconds to be killed. From the time she went out to pass the slower car to the time she was hit and killed is believed to have been around six seconds.

I then move on to statistics informing them that the number one killer among young adults is automobile accidents and how if they use their phone and drive they are four times more likely to get into a car accident.

I end the presentation with a picture of Kelsey. Telling them that the next time they go to pick up their phone while they are driving a car, remember Kelsey and how in six seconds she was gone. Gone because of a phone conversation.

I remember thinking, I did it. It was over. Did I cry? Absolutely and so did many of the students. I knew I had gotten through to some of them.

I have received several messages from students throughout the state since that first presentation. Here are a couple:

I didn't know Kelsey personally but always saw her around school, I remember seeing her and Stacey at the Big Bear a few weeks before the accident and something about her struck me. She seemed like such a bright, happy, caring person. I just recently got my drivers license and told myself that I would not text and drive, but I did it anyway. I missed your presentation at the school and was so upset about it because everyone talked about it for weeks. I couldn't sleep tonight so I decided to spend my time on facebook, something from Kelsey's page popped up so I went and read some things from it. I also watched your video from one of your presentations, I even took my phone out in the beginning to play the game with you and after doing that it finally hit me. I was so busy watching what I was writing that I wasn't watching the video, so I restarted it to see if there was anything I missed. But in life you can't just rewind if your too busy texting and something happens. I just wanted you to know that Kelsey and you both taught me a huge lesson, and I will not text and drive anymore.

Hello Bonnie, I just wanted to say thank you. I just got a phone yesterday and I was driving down the road and was just about to text while I was driving. Then I thought about how last year when you came to the high school and did that presentation about Kelsey and texting and driving. It made me rethink the decision of texting while driving, and I didn't. So, I just wanted to say that you giving this presentation really did help me and who knows it could have possibly saved an accident from happening. Thank you.

Thank you for coming into our school today that was very nice of you..you are changing a lot of peoples lives..I hope a lot of our high schooler's changed their minds about texting and driving because I know I'm never going to text and drive. peace & love.

All schools are special to me but there is one school that really has a huge place in my heart. I was scheduled to do a presentation at Alanson Schools. No one could go with me that day so I went by myself. I don't like doing that because I'm never sure on how I am going to be, but I went. I walked into the school and was greeted by several staff members who were wearing black-and-pink T-shirts that stated "The KDR Challenge Kids Driving Responsibly" and on the back "I Believe". Of course right off the bat I was crying. No other school had ever done that. They didn't know what "Believe" meant to Kelsey and us.

When the students started coming into the gym, they were wearing the same shirts. The teachers, students, and staff of this school were so nice. It was really hard for me to get through the presentation.

This school will forever have a special place in my heart.

It has been a year and a half since that first presentation.

I have changed things up a bit but the message is still there. I have spoken to over seven thousand students and all I can do is pray that I have saved at least one life.

The KDR Challenge website (www.thekdrchallenge.com) has over ten thousand hits on it and that is just in the last year. Her "In Loving Memory" Facebook page has over three thousand likes.

Kelsey's story has been featured on the National Safety Council web page. As a matter of fact, the NSC has become family to me. We work closely together on distracted driving, especially among the teens. Kelsey is part of the Hearts Network which is part of the NSC. I am a board member for the national nonprofit FocusDriven organizations. (www.focusdriven.org) We are advocates for cell free driving. The other board members are parents, family members, friends, and victims of accidents involving cell phones. They all have become my second family. They understand everything I am going through.

One family I have become especially close to is the Teater family.

On January 20, 2004, 12-year-old Joe and his mom were on their way to an after-school activity when a 20-year-old woman ran a red light and slammed into the passenger side of their car, killing Joe. The young lady didn't see the four cars and school bus she passed that were stopped at the red light. She didn't even apply her breaks.

Joe was just a little boy. He had just started middle

Joe Teater

school. He was a funny, loving young man. He loved computers, video games, the school choir, skiing, and church youth groups.

It has been eight years since the Teaters lost Joe, and family functions are still difficult for them. They are huge advocates for cell phone free driving like me. I am honored to call them my friends and I thank them for everything they have done to help me not just getting Kelsey's story out, but for being there for me when I have had bad days, or I read a negative comment about what I am doing. It just saddens me that we had to become friends. By losing a child because of a preventable act.

Kelsey became one of the teens represented in a new campaign AllState insurance is doing. She is featured on the AllState web site. Her story is helping save the lives of many.

I have become involved with the Michigan Office of Highway Safety Planning. It is great being able to work with law enforcement, medical personnel, MDOT employees, etc. We are working together to try and make Michigan roads safer.

Automobile accidents are the leading cause of death among teens. The new drivers are three times more likely to get into an accident than an experienced driver. All drivers are four times more likely to be in an accident if they are using their phone while they drive. Now, take the new driver already at three times more likely to get in an accident and add the phone risk. It is a lethal combination.

Research has shown that the cell phone use and driving are comparible to drinking alcohol and driving. They compared your reaction time when you were using a phone and driving and your reaction time when you had a blood alcohol level of 0.08. They discovered that it was the same. So, using a cell phone and driving is the same as driving with a blood alcohol level of 0.08 and in Michigan that is considered legally drunk. So why do we allow this behavior behind the wheel of a car? There are currently nine states and the District of Columbia that ban the use of handheld devices while driving. What is being missed is that whether you are holding a phone or using a Bluetooth device, it is the same. You are still distracted by the conversation. It is a cognitive issue.

I could write a whole book on the reasons to not use a phone while driving but that is not the purpose of this book. Just know that it is a dangerous act and many, and I mean many, people are being injured or are dying because of it.

We were able to have a bill introduced and passed by the Michigan Senate in 2012. This bill would prevent any driver with a level one or level two driver's license from being able to use a phone while driving. Our district Senator, Howard Walker, had the bill named "Kelsey's Law".

Getting a bill passed is a VERY long process and being so close to the situation, it is very stressful and draining.

The bill was introduced in October, 2011. It was first assigned to the Senate Transportation Committee, but in January, 2012 was moved to the Energy and Technology Committee. Once it was in this committee, it moved quickly. I traveled to Lansing and testified in front of the Senate Energy and Technology Committee. What an experience! I wasn't nervous that day. I had the knowledge of the dangers of using a phone and driving, I had my Kelsey's story, but most of all, I had an angel on my shoulder. I had God with me. Did I cry? Absolutely. It was just a hearing that day. They voted on whether to pass it on to the Senate for a vote the following week. I was unable to make that vote, but the Chair of the committee, Senator Nofs, e-mailed and informed me that it had passed the committee.

wireless
TEAM WIRELESS | Premium Retailer
OPEN
WE SUPPORT
KELSEY S
LAW

Chapter 11: Kelsey's Law

It was a couple weeks later that I received an e-mail from Senator Walker saying the Senate was going to vote on the bill. I did make it to that and it passed the Senate 28 – 10. The ten that voted against the bill stated that they wanted the bill to be for everyone and not just the students. This bill passed the Senate in the morning and was introduced into the House that afternoon. This was March 2012.

There the bill sat for nine months. In the House Transportation Committee. I sent e-mail after e-mail to the Chair of the committee and the Speaker of the House. No response. Nothing.

In September 2012, I decided to hold a press conference on the capitol steps in Lansing. With the help of the National Safety Council and FocusDriven, we were able to get several supporters to speak at the press conference. There were several news agencies there and several people standing in support of the bill. We thought it was a great turn out.

But, once again, no movement on the bill. I once again sent an e-mail to the Speaker of the House and this time I e-mailed the entire Transportation Committee. I simply asked them "Why? Why didn't we have a hearing like we were promised months earlier? Why?" Two days later I received an e-mail from Senator Walker's staffer, Eric. He informed me that we had a hearing. December 5, 2012. Finally, I was going to be able to talk to the Transportation Committee and get them to vote yes on the bill so it would go to the House floor. There was only one problem, this was the Lame Duck period and we only had one week to get it through. How was I going to do this?

Throughout the process of working on the bill, I have made several friends. These friends contact their friends, and so on. Through social networking I have been able to gain a lot of support. Support from students that the bill will affect to all law enforcement agencies, the Michigan Municipal League, several health care agencies, and several insurance companies.

As I was trying to figure out my strategy on getting the bill moving in a week, Through e-mail I met Kevin McKinney from a lobbying firm in Lansing. He asked me if I had a PR firm to which I said no. I told him I do all the contacting of media, supporters, etc. A few minutes later he e-mailed me and told me that Kelly from Truscott Rossman the largest PR firm in Michigan would be contacting me to help get the bill through the Lame Duck time, pro bono. I cried because I was so run down and tired from the stress of trying to get the bill going. If we didn't get the bill passed by the end of the year, the bill would die and we would have to start all over again.

I spoke to Kelly from the PR firm later that evening and she told me to get ready and hold on because we were going to be on a fast ride. Fast ride was an understatement. Over the next couple weeks leading up to the hearing, I did more interviews for newspapers and radio shows than I had done in the last nine months. We put pressure on the Speaker of the House as he was the one holding up the bill. We had another press conference where several TV and

> *Why? Why didn't we have a hearing like we were promised?*

newspaper reporters came. Once again I had several supporters speak at the press conference. There was a web page set up; we pushed for people to e-mail their legislator; and used Facebook and Twitter to push out the message.

Ronnie and I traveled to Lansing on the Monday before the hearing and spoke to about a thousand students in Reed City in the morning and then traveled on to Lansing for the press conference that afternoon. I was scheduled to do four radio interviews Tuesday morning, starting at 6:30 a.m. But

I had the afternoon off so I decided to go to the capitol and do some lobbying outside the House floor. Kevin from the lobbying firm met me there and taught me how to do it. I was able to get all the Representatives on the Transportation Committee to come out and speak to me. I didn't think they would, but they did. They were all very nice. I gave them some information on distracted driving and a postcard that had Kelsey's picture on it and her story.

Wednesday came. We anticipated several people to be there to either testify or just sit with us to show support for the bill. There were so many supporters there that an overflow room had to be opened for people to sit in and watch the hearing on TV's.

Senator Walker testified first. I sat next to him. It was my time. I testified and at the end I knew that we did EVERY-THING we could do to get them to move the bill out of the committee and onto the house floor. After the hearing, I was able to speak to the Chair of the committee and he stated he was thinking on voting it out of committee next week. That would make it the last week of Lame Duck.

It is in God's hands. We just have to "BELIEVE".

Ronnie and I arrived home Wednesday night. We were both really tired. Thursday was a rough day for me. I cried most of the day as I was so tired. I also had received an e-mail stating that the committee was going to vote on the bill the last week of Lame Duck which would put the bill at the last step, on the floor of the house. BUT, the speaker once again stated he will NOT let there be a vote on the bill.

It is in God's hands. We just have to "BELIEVE".

How can this be? How can one person decide whether this will be law or not? If he doesn't like the bill, why can't he just vote no but let the other representatives vote what they want. I could handle the house not passing it, but one person stopping the whole process with all the support we have for the bill just doesn't seem right.

The Monday after I testified I received an e-mail from the PR firm. The Chair of the Transportation Committee wanted her to get in touch with me to let me know that there would NOT be a hearing on Tuesday to vote on the bill. He apologized to her several times and told her that Kelsey's Law was one of the bills on his top priority list to get on to the house floor by the end of Lame Duck. This didn't surprise me.

But, once again it is in God's hands. We just have to "BELIEVE".

On the last day of what they call the Lame Duck session, I received a call from my Senator and was told the speaker of the house said he would introduce the bill for a vote IF we could generate enough votes for it to pass. We were able to do that.

BELIEVE

I sat watching the last house session for the year on my computer, praying so hard for a vote. I tried to stay positive and "Believe" but it was so hard. This had been such a long journey; one I really didn't want to take again, but would if the bill didn't pass.

The day was like a roller-coaster ride. One minute good news, next minute not so good news. The session went into the wee hours of the morning. I was still watching it online lying in my bed refusing to go to sleep. I was using e-mail, Facebook, phone calls, and texts to communicate with everyone in Lansing. My state Representative was even texting me from the floor of the House. A little after 12 a.m. I received word that the bill that was in the Senate that the House wanted to pass, passed. The deal now was the House had to discharge my bill from the Transportation Committee and allow it to go to a vote. An hour went by and finally the bill was discharged from committee. We were one step closer. Finally at 1:45 a.m., the Michigan House, voted on SB 756. It passed, 74 to 33. I was so excited I couldn't cry at first. I felt like I was in a dream. We had worked so hard for this day and I couldn't believe it was finally here.

My Facebook blew up with messages, my phone was ringing off the wall and I kept getting text after text after text. I think my last phone call came in a little after 3 a.m. But at around 5:30 a.m., it started up again.

I e-mailed the speaker of the house and told him, "Thank you." I stated that he doesn't realize how many lives this will save. And I told him that I was crying happy tears for the first time in three years.

"BELIEVE"

I have to say that Eric Dean and Senator Howard Walker are the best. They have stood by this bill from day one. They have worked so hard to get it passed. I tell them all the time how much I appreciate it, but I don't think they really know how much. Kelsey would be so proud of them. I can see her saying, "I love those guys mom." And she would mean it.

Gov. Rick Snyder signed Kelsey's Law in Lansing on Tuesday, January 8, 2013, surrounded by the Raffaele family — Bonnie, Courtney, and Ron.

Chapter 12:
The Signing

On January 8, 2013 Ronnie, Courtney and myself traveled to Lansing, Michigan for the signing of the bill. The Governor's office asked me if I wanted a public or private signing. I thought for a few minutes and then told them a public one. I had so many people that worked on getting the bill passed and so many news outlets that had followed me through this process and I felt they needed to be there to see it through to the end.

The signing was to take place at 3:00 p.m. Eric Dean, from Senator Walker's office, asked me to be at their office around 2:30 p.m. We left early that morning; I wanted to arrive in plenty of time.

At 2:40 p.m. we made our way to the Governor's office. I wasn't nervous at all. Even though he was the Governor, he was still a human being and most importantly he was a father. As a matter of fact, he has a daughter named Kelsey who is sixteen and just received her driver's license a few months ago.

When we arrived Darren, the governor's aide, was at the check point waiting for us. I have to say he is a really nice man. We made it through security along with Senator Walker and Eric. Once we were upstairs, we were taken into a really nice room where we were greeted by another one of the Governor's workers. She explained that we could leave our belongings there and retrieve them after the signing. She took Ronnie, Courtney and I in to meet the Governor. We hugged and I thanked him for signing the bill. After chatting for a bit, we took a picture of us with him and then we were taken to a conference room. We were with Senator Walker, Eric, and other law enforcement representatives. We were told how we were going to proceed to the media room, who would speak, and in what order.

Within a few minutes we were whisked down a narrow hall and stairs to a door that was outside the media room. The Governor informed us we would go in as soon as the Secret Service said it was okay. Yes, the Secret Service. They don't smile much. I just wanted to give them a hug. But I didn't.

They gave the okay to go in and opened the door. We walked in - it was so surreal. You see it on TV all the time, but actually being there, walking out with the Governor for a press conference was unbelievable. All the cameras clicking and all the people. Just amazing. I was so glad Courtney was there to experience it.

The Governor spoke first, then Senator Walker, and then I said just a few words. The Governor went to the desk and signed the bill into law. I remember crying some as he signed it, just amazed that we did it. We are able to save lives. Kelsey would be so happy.

I was told before I went to the signing, by several people, to get the pen that he signed the bill with. There were four pens on the table so I was watched to see which one he

It was all so surreal.

used. But, he used all of them. There were four copies of the bill and he used a pen for each one. So, I got all four pens.

After the signing we took several pictures and then the Governor was whisked away. The press was after me for interviews, but Darren informed them they could talk to me downstairs and he whisked Courtney, Ronnie and I away. It was nice having someone else be in charge of the media. I had held press conferences in Lansing on the bill and I was always the one in charge. Nice not to be this time. Besides, I was trying to take it all in. It was like I was in a dream.

We retrieved our belongings and went downstairs. The media was there and they surrounded me and asked several questions. I was used to this so it didn't bother me.

On the way home my phone kept ringing. Facebook pages were blowing up. Twitter was going crazy. We just couldn't believe that it was done. We had "Kelsey's Law".

The next day it was all over the internet, newspapers throughout the US, and on TV stations. It was just overwhelming.

One journey complete but so much more work to do. I hadn't smiled so much and I hadn't been so happy in three years. It was a good day.

This is the press release from the Governor's office:

LANSING, Mich. - Gov. Rick Snyder today signed Kelsey's Law to help protect Michigan's young, inexperienced drivers and other motorists.

Senate Bill 756, sponsored by state Sen. Howard Walker, bans cellphone use for anyone driving on a level 1 or level 2 graduated driver license in Michigan.

The new law is named in honor of Kelsey Raffaele, 17, of Sault Ste. Marie, who died tragically in a cellphone-related automobile crash in 2010.

"This law means a lot to me, both as governor and as a parent of a young person who is learning to drive," Snyder said. "I appreciate the efforts of Kelsey's mother, Bonnie, and family who have worked tirelessly to get the message out about the dangers of distracted driving. We should be doing everything we can to make sure beginning drivers are focused on learning how to drive. I believe this law will help them gain that experience while reinforcing their responsibilities behind the wheel."

The new law allows for primary enforcement by police, though in most cases it will be enforced after the detection of another moving violation. A violation of the law will result in a civil infraction to be determined by the local jurisdiction. No points will be assigned to the driver's record and drivers will not be punished for using a vehicle's integrated hands-free phone system or for using cell phones to report an emergency.

Cell phones and other distractions exacerbate a young driver's inexperience and lead to more traffic crashes, which are the No. 1 killer of teens.

Michigan adopted a statewide ban on texting-while-driving in 2010.

SB 756 is now Public Act 592 of 2012 and will take effect in late march.

I just really looked at this. "SB 756 is now Public Act 592." Courtney and Kelsey were born 5/92. It was another sign from God.

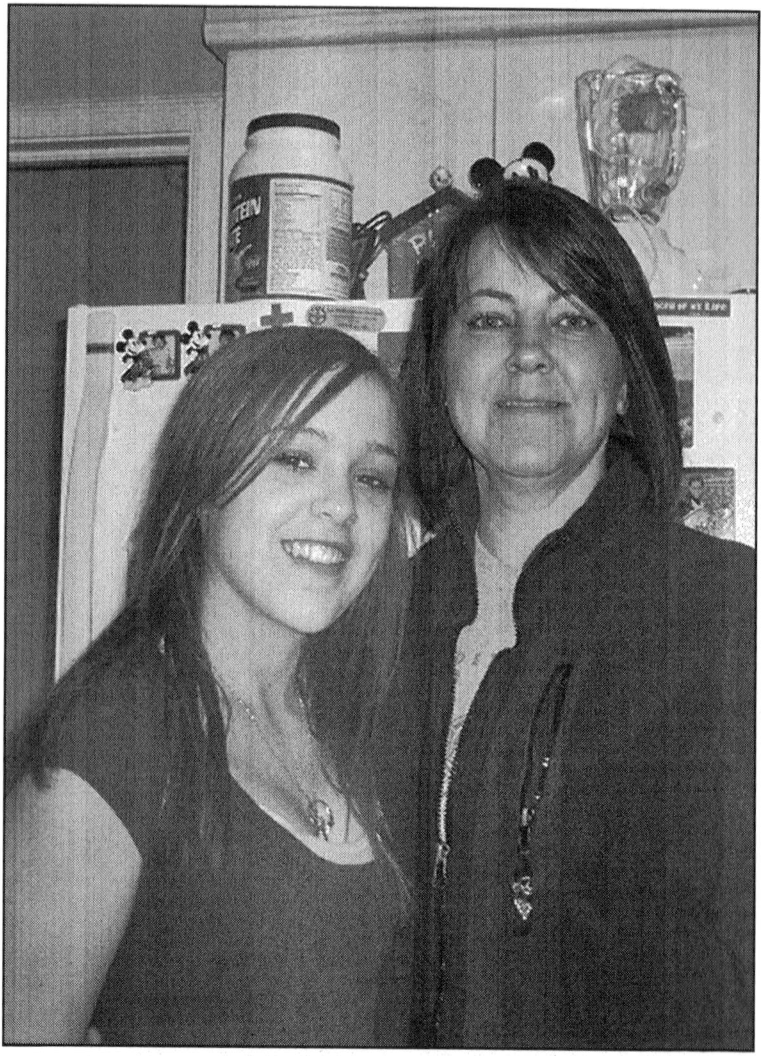

Chapter 13: Questioning God

I wondered if Kelsey was happy with what I was doing. Was she mad because I talk about her using her phone? Could she see how I was trying to do what I thought she would do? Did she know how much I love her and how much I missed her? I knew these were 'human' feelings, but I am human. I asked my preacher. This is what he said:

I can only tell you what the Bible says, because that is where true comfort comes.

Hebrews 12:1 says; "Since we have so great a cloud of witnesses...." The author is talking about deceased believers listed in Hebrews 11 (which is the Hall of Faith).

Those people — believers who have passed, like Kelsey -— know and see what's going on here. Which tells me, Kelsey DOES know and understand everything you just wrote to me. She knows you are still taking care of her and trying to save others and to keep her memory alive. She is your "witness" in Heaven as from Hebrews 12:1.

Bonnie, Kelsey DOES know how much you love her and miss her so deeply. Though Kelsey feels deeply about your broken heart, if she cries God Himself is wiping away all her tears with His own hand, Revelation 21:4.

Revelation 21:4; "God will wipe away every tear from their eyes; and there will no longer be any death; there will no longer be any mourning, or crying, or pain; the first

> **Go ahead, read these scriptures and BELIEVE that Kelsey knows, cares about all you and Ron are doing for her.**

things have passed away."

Personally, I believe that God will send a guardian angel to hug you for Kelsey. About guardian angels see Hebrews 1:13-14

"Are they (angels) not all ministering spirits, sent out to render service for the sake of those who will inherit salvation?"

Or, it may be the Holy Spirit, the Father, or Jesus, in my opinion.

Go ahead, read these scriptures and BELIEVE that Kelsey knows, cares about all you and Ron are doing for her. That will warm her heart and will help heal yours as well.

That is what the Bible teaches me about these topics. I've preached all this for decades, this is not new teaching to me. It's the truth! All done through the grace of God through Calvary and the sacrifice of Jesus and His bodily resurrection from the dead.

I know it may seem silly but just knowing that Kelsey knew everything I was trying to do made me feel much better. I know it isn't important in Heaven, but I'm not there yet. I am still on this earth as a human being. A mother trying to make sense out of losing her daughter.

I know that I am supposed to be saving lives by telling them about Kelsey and the danger of using cell phone while driving. But I still felt as though I was missing something. I am supposed to be doing more. I believe that I am supposed to not only speak about the dangers of using a phone while driving, but I am supposed to lead people to Christ through Kelsey's story. Why, you may ask. Because my daughter has lead me closer to Christ since her death. I need to "save" the lives of people who don't "Believe". Just like Kelsey did in her own little way while she was alive.

The night of the accident I kept asking the nurses if they had taken a ring of Kelsey's. A silver one with stars on it and "Believe" inscribed on the inside. They kept telling me they didn't find that ring. I was frantic. I had to have that ring because it was one of the last things I bought her. I remember when she read what was inside and asked if she needed to believe in herself more. I told her yes and that she had to remember to believe in God and do right.

It was sometime during the week after she passed away that we were told that the car had been released by the police and we could go and get Kelsey's personal belongings from the vehicle. Ronnie and I couldn't do it so I asked my friend, the state trooper, if she could go and get it for me. She did. She brought her purse to the house. I remember asking her if she had looked for the ring. I had searched her room and asked everyone if they knew where it was. There in the zipper part of her purse was the ring. I still have that ring around my neck on a chain with another charm that says "Believe" on it and a cross. I will NEVER take it off.

> **I have told the kids and others since Kelsey's passing that they have to "Believe" in order to see her again.**

I have told the kids and others since Kelsey's passing that they have to "Believe" in order to see her again. They have brought several things to Kelsey's grave with "Believe" on it. I even got a tattoo, yes a tattoo, on my foot with the same stars as her ring and the word "Believe."

Kelsey's favorite scripture was Philippians 4:13 "I can do

all things through Christ who gives me strength." I knew this, but what I didn't know was that she quoted that scripture to some of her friends when they were having problems.

One of Kelsey's classmates wrote the following:

Strength: as you know, Kelsey is the type of girl who leaves a lasting impression on others. 2010 was the hardest year of my life and ended up to be a real test of my inner strength. I remember receiving the call on January 24th. I didn't want to believe it. The next few weeks were so hard. I began questioning my faith and God himself. Kelsey was such an amazing girl: beautiful, happy, strong, confident, intelligent, inspirational, and friendly. She had such strong faith, so what could God's reason be? It was hard to see her empty seat in Mrs. Harrington's class day after day. We would set time aside in class to talk and share storied about her. I kept reminding myself Kelsey was never far. She may not be here physically but she is here, in all of our hearts. A short three weeks later our school lost Talon, and in May by brother was put into a coma. By this time I was emotionally exhausted and I had nothing left to give. I let my grades slip, I struggled to get myself to come to school, and I was in no way prepared to take my exams, but Kelsey kept me going. I was prepared to fail geometry and retake it the following year, when I had a conversation with a very good friend. She reminded me of this quote and how disappointed Kel would have been if she was there. I could just hear Kelsey's voice in my head that day "I can do all things through Him who strengthens me". In that moment I no longer felt as though failing was an option. I found the strength to pull myself together and make it through the last few weeks of school I passed all of my classes and went into that summer with a new positive attitude.

> ***We didn't realize what an impact her death had on everyone.***

So you see Kelsey was doing God's work even though in today's society, especially with teens, it isn't the 'cool' thing to do. But that was Kel. When she believed in something she would do whatever it took to stand up for her belief.

We didn't realize what an impact her death had on everyone, not just the kids, until months/years later. People we didn't even know in this community have told us how she has impacted their life. People that drive by the crash site every day on their way to work and say hi to Kel as they drive by or they stop and just say a prayer there.

On May 2, 1992 God blessed me with two beautiful baby girls. He allowed me to have Kelsey on this earth for seventeen years, eight months and 22 wonderful days. What a blessing. He trusted me to teach them about Him. I would tell them how He died on the cross so we could have eternal life. Although there were times that I drifted away from this, God always knew I would come back to Him. I thank God for trusting in me. I thank Him for giving me Kelsey and Courtney. Even if I only had Kelsey for a short time, what a wonderful time it was. She brought such joy into our home and hearts. I will see her again someday. God has promised us that.

John 3:16 "Whoever believes in me shall not perish but have everlasting life."

Kelsey is in Heaven waiting for us all to be together once again.

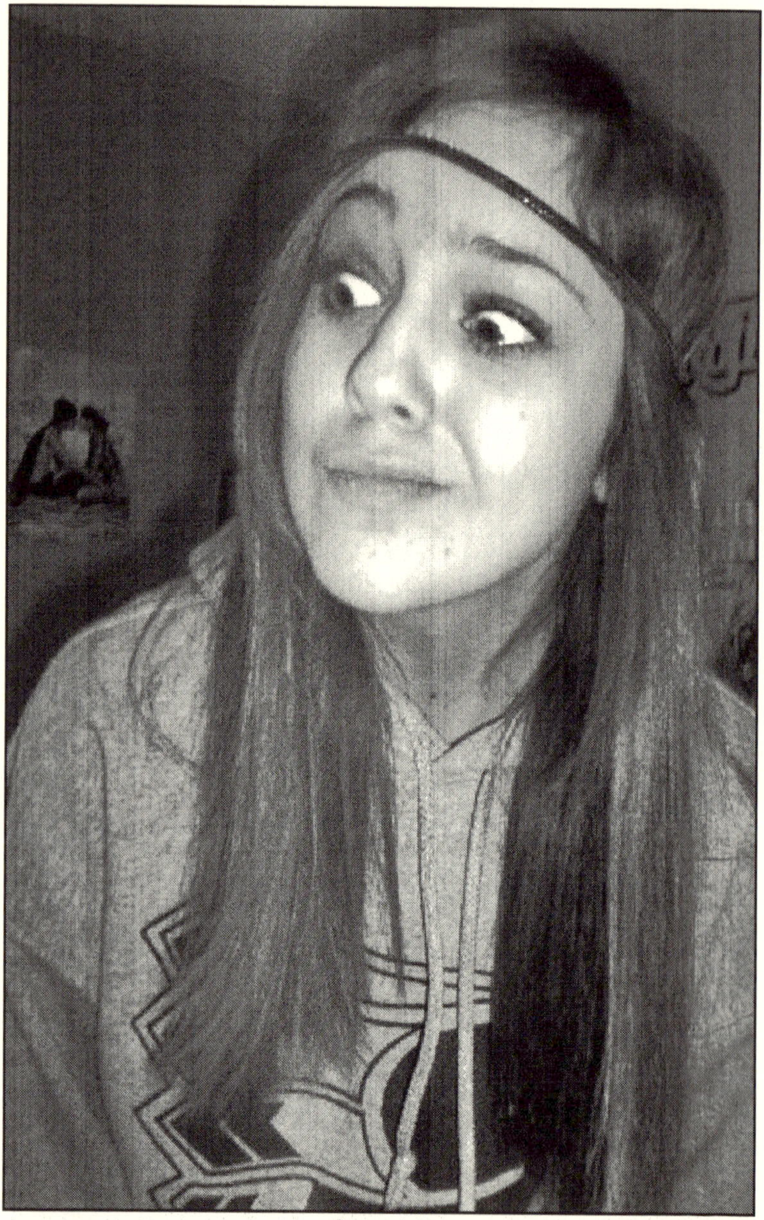

Chapter 14:
In Her Own Words

Kelsey wrote a lot. I think it helped her cope with things. Like I hope writing this book will help me cope with her death.

It was about a year after Kelsey passed away when Courtney was going through files on Kelsey's computer and looking at her MySpace account. Courtney stumbled upon the following entry:

"It's unbelievable to know how much I've been through in my life time. Having friends pass away within just one year. I've been knocked down so many times and I'm surprised that I'm still standing on my own two feet. Since the many tragic death issues I've experienced I look at death in a different way. Have you ever wondered if the ones who you lost being; mother, father, brother, sister, cousin, friend, aunt, uncle, grandparents, whatever it is.. do they just look down on you, the ones they loved or do they see the whole world? People they've never know or even met. I use to take things in life for granted like for the loving family I've been

blessed with, the town I live in, everything. I can now say I'm thankful. I'm thankful for being able to walk outside my front door without the fear of being shot to death. Or taking summer walks without the fear of being jumped. Many people take death in different ways. Some do not believe in the afterlife, as for me I do. Who's the one that keeps me strong when I am upset, who talks to me every night as I lie awake crying in my room, who watches over me and makes me feel safe and protected. Not only with God's help I have my angels help. Brett being the main one. Call it crazy talk, or whatever you like. I recently watched the movie "Freedom Writers" in my english class this past week. Watching that movie made me think.. think about my life and other things as well. I then looked up some more information on the internet to learn more about these kids. I come to find out a kid who starred in the movie Armand Jones played "Grant Rice" was shot just after filming the movie. He never got to see himself in that movie. I then read a little more about him. Coming to his myspace page. No, I did not know this kid, never even talked to him, or seen him in person. But I feel something close with him. He was a strong believer in God. He loved to rap & was a great dancer. I don't know where I am going with this but reading his story of his death made me sad.. a bit upset. Those kids out there have gone through so much in life, its amazing how many of them make it to the age of 18. How would you like to go out and have fun then the next thing you know you or your friend is lying on the ground with a bullet in their chest. I guess my point to this blog is..Live your life every day, have fun every day, and enjoy it while you can because you never know when your last day will come.....kdr"

She states in here how she lies in her bed at night and talks to Brett and God. I now lie in HER bed and talk to her and God. It is surreal the things that I now do that she did. And, I started doing these things before we found the writings where she talks about doing them. It is like we are still connected even though she is in Heaven.

Look at how she signed this letter. KDR. Exactly what I named her non-profit, the KDR Challenge. I didn't see this writing until after I came up with the KDR Challenge. Once again, like we are still connected even though she is in Heaven.

Kelsey and her Dad were the best of friends. She LOVED him and I mean really LOVED him. This is a file entitled, "Dad & Kels inside jokes" Kelsey had on her computer. Here are their sayings they were fond of repeating.

Turtle Soup

Baby where are you? Bam!!!

Happy Easter

Dad, you don't listen!

Why so glum chum?

Dad I just can't see ya

Why so blue lou?

WHERE ARE YOU!?

Dad, where are you... can't see ya... There ya are.

Dad, what are ya doin?

I just love you

You're weird

Whatd ya help?

DAD

You're my best friend

Daddy doesn't listen to puppy, puppy doesn't listen to daddy, ANYMORE

After she had passed away I wanted to have a quilt made of her blue jeans. My friend, Sophie said she would make it for me. Sophie, also is really good at embroidery. Her daughter knew Kelsey had a lot of sayings and suggested Sophie embroider them on the jeans. What a great idea. So, we were franticly trying to remember all the sayings she would say. Well, Courtney stumbled upon this file on Kelsey's computer, why she created it I will never know, but thank God she did. We were able to have Sophie embroider them on the quilt.

Not only did we find writings on Kelsey's computer or social networking sites, but we found writings on walls down stairs, notes in class notebooks that you would one day turn the page and there it was, and notes in cars. It is almost like she knew something was going to happen to her and wanted us to find these things and laugh. She would leave her dad notes at his work and me notes at my office at the high school. I still have all the notes. She even wrote this one using paint on my computer. When I came to my desk, there it was up on my screen.

I have this one note that says "Gwen Renee Stefani is my best friend!" Kelsey LOVED Gwen. And I mean she really LOVED her. I have a video of Kelsey singing "Walking in a Spider Web" and "I'm Just a Girl" while Ronnie was playing it on the keyboards. And, Kelsey was only three or four years old. Kelsey's favorite perfume was LAMB. Her bedroom door and closet door was, and still is, covered with Gwen pictures from magazines. I had to purchase anything I could find and afford, of Gwen.

When Gwen went on tour with her solo album she came to Michigan. I got up early the day the tickets went on sale and went to my friend's house. Kelsey didn't know I was purchasing tickets. We had five computers set up and when the tickets went on sale, we yelled the section and seats we got. I picked the best ones and purchased them. I than went back home and woke Kelsey up telling her we were going to see Gwen. You would have thought I gave her a million dollars she was so excited.

On the day of the concert Kelsey was able to see Gwen's bus outside the auditorium. She was so excited, and of course I took her picture by it. We purchased several items from the merchandise they were selling. We had to have it.

The opening act finished and we are waiting for Gwen to come on. Kelsey was in middle school so she was about twelve years old. The band starts playing and Kelsey starts crying. The curtain hadn't even gone up. It was at that moment I knew that the two-hundred dollars I spent on tickets was worth it.

I don't think Kelsey stopped smiling the whole concert. She was so excited and happy that even though we weren't that close, she was still in the same room as her idol.

Even up until the day Kelsey died, she idolized Gwen. She waited for Gwen's babies to be born. She had to know their names and everything else about them. Like I said her room is still filled with pictures of her. Her dream was to actually meet Gwen and talk to her. She had that dream as far back as when she was singing Gwen's songs at the age of three or four.

Since Kelsey passed away I have put it at the top of my bucket list to meet Gwen. I feel the need to tell her about

Kelsey and how Kelsey adored her. I need to thank Gwen for being such a good inspiration and role model for my daughter. I can only hope that someday I will get that chance.

One day Courtney, Ronnie and I were at West Pier eating supper. It was a little over a year after Kelsey had passed away. Ronnie has this habit of cleaning cars, so as we were waiting for our food to come, he was cleaning the car. He came upon this little notebook and there was a note from Kelsey. It said, "Dad, I know if you find this you are cleaning the car."

We all started laughing and crying at the same time. I could feel her with us that day.

Courtney was in school one day about three or four weeks after Kelsey had passed when she opened her note book and found the following note from Kelsey. "Court, you were right, you're always right. Screw hockey players. Love You Kel"

The most meaningful writing I found of Kel's was the one she wrote entitled,

"Story of my Life".

Intro....

The worst quality I see in myself is I forgive others way

too easily, but for most of you, that's a good thing. I'm vulnerable to believing lies but I hate being lied to. I make up excuses for everything and blame other people for my problems. I don't get too close to people, because I fear that I'll be let down in the end, which in most cases I am. I'm old enough to know better and young enough to not care. I've been to hell and back and I'm still standing strong. I fake a smile and pretend everything's okay when really it isn't. I'm not perfect and never will be. I don't care if you judge me because judgment is something that I will never be able to run away from. What we complain about in life is what life revolves around. There's no point in escaping it. So, why try? I'm not easy to understand, easy to make friends with, but hard to keep around. I've gone through more than most have gone through their whole lives. I feel like I've lost everything that has ever mattered to me. I don't ask for sympathy. I ask for you to understand me. I'm losing faith in everyone including myself. I love life, but it's beginning to let me down just like everyone else. Constantly being put down, constantly getting hurt. But I try to pull through with a smile on my face. I'll admit, I have done some pretty crazy stuff in my life time. Getting into the wrong crowd and such. After this summer passed I realized I don't need that kind of stuff in my life anymore it was just causing more pain than I already had. Why do we always seem to think we can trust our "best friends"? When in reality, everyone knows you can't really trust anyone but YOURSELF. I try hard to be the so called "nice guy" in situations...but it's really hard when your best friends betray you...I'm not saying I'm not mean, because yes I can be, just as well as everyone else. I'm beginning to realize a lot of things in life...Although I'm still learning how to deal with the "drama" we have. I can't stand when people tell you your boyfriends are "just friends" or here's one of my favorites "he's like my brother" c'mon get real we all know you have or had feelings for him at one point in time. Especially when you repeat yourself. I never really took much action when it came to boyfriends "hooking up" with my friends or even other girls for that matter. I wasn't really a strong person, couldn't really stick up for myself. But now after all the stuff I've been through I'm learning and progressing. I don't understand why girls LOVE the attention to fight. Don't take this in a wrong way...I'm not pointing out anyone in particular...It just makes me wonder why? Why do you like to stir things up so much? Why do you seem to think you have to bring other people into our business? Sometimes I can't be true to myself, I tend to tell myself not to do something and then end up doing it. But everyone does. Oh well. Through all the boyfriends I've had and the mistakes I made with them I'm glad to say that I've stayed strong through it all and I now know what guys I'm looking for next. I'm sick of being disrespected when it comes to relationships. I always seem to be the one taken advantage of. In the words of my dad "its time to move on". And I'm more ready than ever. Bring it on. So this so called "gangster act" – immature. Enough said. At least I'm admitting it. Everyone goes through different phases in life, I guess that was just one of mine.

My Life...

Well I think the first paragraph explained a lot. In this section, I'm starting from day one..

May 2, 1992 I was born 2nd after my twin sister Courtney. We grew up in a great home, raised by two wonderful parents. Never had troubles or family problems. Growing up was always fun, especially having a sister around. My mom always use to dress us up in matching outfits, I always

got a kick out of that. Most people compared me and my sister with the Olsen twins. I would always be Mary-Kate, she would be Ashley. I wasn't really sure how that went. It was nice knowing I had someone always there. In fact, our first year without being in the same class killed me, I just wanted to be with my sister I guess. I looked up to her a lot in our younger days, I do now as well. I guess you could say we were a typical, average American family just like everyone else. My mom loved working with computers and technology. My dad was more of a motor-pooling type of guy. He worked up at the college. Middle school is where I started my troublesomeness (if that's what you would like to call it). Around 7th grade, I was age 12, I got in with the wrong crowd. Although I never really did anything too bad up until I hit high school, my freshmen year. People say at age 13 is where young kids start with the bad habits. Not for me. My freshmen year was basically a blur. I don't remember much. I do remember one of the most tragic days I had to go through on February 22, 2007 one of my best friends, former boyfriend, Brett Barancik passed away from cancer. We knew it was coming, we just didn't know it was that quick. He was diagnosed with cancer at age 11 in the 5th grade. That following summer another one my close friends Charles "Chucky" Hughes passed away due to a swimming accident. As you could tell that wasn't a bright year for me. Onto my sophomore year is when things started to get rough. Everyone falls in love right? Well I happened to fall in love with not a very good person for me. Especially at the age of 15, my first heartbreak. I started dating this kid over the summer of '07. He was included in the "wrong crowd" I had been associated with throughout my freshmen year. It was obvious we had our "party" times, which wasn't a good thing for me in the end. Long story short, I came to find out this kid "I was in love with" wasn't right for me. We had our problems, our fights, you know, typical teenage boyfriend & girlfriend stuff. After a year of being pushed around I realized I didn't need a lying, cheating, abusive guy like him. It was time to move on. Summer 08 rolled on. At this point I didn't know how to handle myself. I was so heartbroken by the fact of me not being with this kid anymore. I didn't really understand why I loved him so much. We had rough times, my parents didn't approve so it made it worse for us to even see each other. We were lucky we got to see each other *once a week. Eventually I sucked it up and got him out of my head and met another kid. I've known this guy for about three years now. We met through my cousin a while back on a trip down to Cadillac. He originally lived in Cadillac but moved up to play hockey. So we decided to get together, try things out. Well I came to find out he was like the last. Now, I haven't had just two boyfriends in my life. These two were just major ones, the ones I actually fell hard for, or as I would like to put it "fell in love with." By this relationship I was just so sick of getting hurt all the time. I thought I was never good enough for anyone. Why was I always getting hurt? Of course yet again, my parents did not approve. The reason being he was a "heart breaker" and they just didn't wanna see me get hurt again. I understood completely why they wouldn't allow us to be with each other because they didn't wanna see me go through what I went through with the last heart break. It's crazy to say I experienced my first heart break at age 15 when most experience after the age of 20. Now my junior year, things are still rough. I'm trying to stay clean from now on. I can happily say I've been clean for a very long time, longer than I would have expected. Hopefully things will get better for me. I'm trying to stay positive and not look at the negative side so much. We'll see how life goes on. Until then...you're amazing if you read all this. Much love,*

xoxo kels

Heroes.......

My cousin.

I've had many friends that have been there for me through everything especially all the hard times I've gone through. The most important person to me would have to be my cousin Brock. He was the only one that actually showed me he cared about my feelings and my problems. Every time I would get upset he'd be the one I called. He was always there for me through thick and thin and I can still call him any time of the day and he'll be there to listen. Knowing you have someone there by your side through everything you go through is one of the greatest feelings in the world. I'm lucky to have experienced that feeling with Brock. He means so much to me, and has never let me down. He taught me a lot in life. I appreciate him and everything he has done for me.

My mom.

    I've deff. had my ups and downs throughout the past few years of my life. I've done some pretty messed up *things. I've upset my mom by the choices I made and she still believed in me and stayed with me through it all. I thank her for never giving up on me, and knowing that someday I would "get better" and change my ways. I love you Ma!*

My dad.

My dad has always been there for me through thick and thin. Still is today. He's been my best friend since the 6th grade and still is. He always knows how to put a smile on my face when I'm upset. He's helped me stay strong through all the mistakes I've made. I thank him for everything he has done for me, I love you Dad!

My Twin:

It is fun being a twin. We do a lot together. I don't know what I would do without her. She has always been there for me. We have done some silly things together. Whenever I need advice on boys, I ask Courtney and she is always right. I love you Courtney!

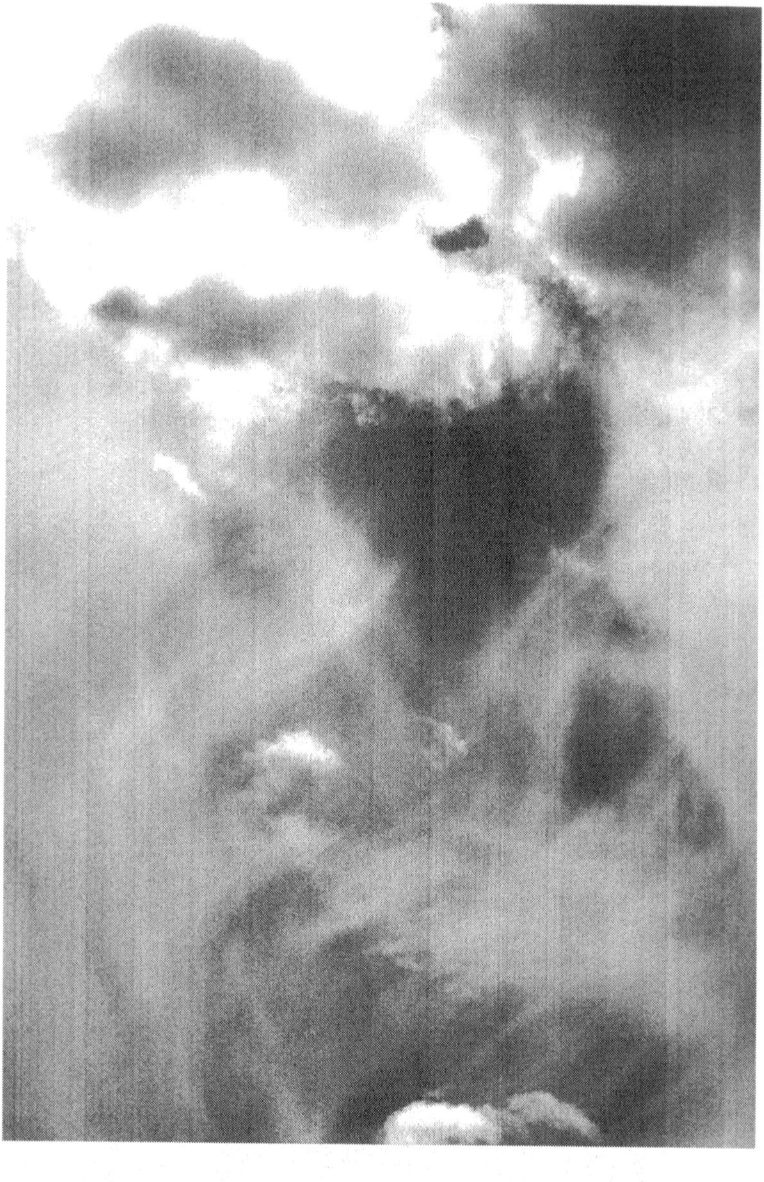

Chapter 15:
Signs from God

It has been almost three years now and I cry every day of my life. I miss her so much. My heart is forever broken. I tried so hard to have a child. All I ever wanted in life was to be a mom. When I finally had my girls, I was the happiest person in the world. I did everything with them. I even gave up a good job at one school district and took a huge pay cut to work in the same school district they were in. What more could a mom ask for than to go to work and see her children all day and then go home with them? What more could a mom ask for than to have summers off with her children and be able to do so much with them? I was in Heaven. I couldn't ask for anything more.

Then to have my world ripped away from me in just six seconds? I can't tell you how much that hurts.

I sleep in her bed a lot. I sleep where she did when she was talking to God and her friend Brett – who passed away too young as well. I now talk to God and her. I sleep the best when I am in her bed. It's like I can feel her or an angel or God with me and hugging me as I lay there. It is the most peaceful feeling.

I believe that God sends signs to let us know our loved ones are safe with Him.

Here are just a few that I have experienced.

I go to her grave all the time. I love just lying there and listening to music and looking up into the sky. I even go there during the winter and make snow angels and heart shapes in the snow. One winter I was feeling really down. I was at her grave sitting... crying. I was getting cold so I laid down to make a snow angel. I looked up into the sky and saw a rainbow. Yes, in the dead of winter, a rainbow. I knew it was a sign from God that everything was going to be okay and Kelsey was safe with Him. You see, there is a song that came out after Kelsey passed from The Band Perry. It's called, "If I Die Young." One of the lines in the song says,

Lord make me a rainbow,

To shine down on my mother

She'll know I'm safe with you

When she stands under my colors."

I had listened to that song when I was there that day.

One summer day I looked up into the sky and there among the clouds was a heart shape made out of the blue sky. I knew it was another sign from the Lord, telling me He was there and everything was going to be okay.

I'm not the only one that has had signs. The first Father's Day after Kelsey passed away, Ronnie got up and to his sur-

Kelsey and Courtney

prise was greeted by a groundhog on the back deck looking in the sliding doors.

To understand the groundhog's encounter, here is the story.

One summer we had a momma groundhog and a baby groundhog in the back yard. Ronnie tried with all his might to kill them, but couldn't. He would try to shoot them and miss. It was the joke of the house for several weeks that summer. We called him "Elmer Fudd!"

Kelsey especially had a ball teasing him over not being

> *"I can do all things through Christ who strengthens me."*

able to get the groundhogs.

So you see to have that groundhog up on the deck looking in the window was a sign. We had never had a groundhog on the deck before and to this day there has never been another one. Not even one in the backyard.

Kelsey's favorite scripture was Philippians 4:13, "I can do all things through Christ who strengthens me."

Each year for Kelsey's Scholarship, Sault High students — going to LSSU — apply for the scholarship by writing an essay stating why they believe they deserve the scholarship. The third year as we were deciding on the recipient, a young lady talked about how Kelsey used to recite Philippians 4:13 to her when she was having a tough time. It brought tears to my eyes that my daughter, at the age of 15 or 16, was quoting scripture to her friends.

I listen to Christian music all the time. One day I was listening to Matthew West's song, "Strong Enough." The bridge of the song is that scripture. To me it's another sign that it is going to be okay and I'm "Strong Enough." With God's help I/we are strong enough to get through this. Kelsey's friends sent this same quote right after she passed away. They told me that Kel used to tell them it all the time.

Kelsey told them, "You were only given this life because you are strong enough to live it."

Who would have ever thought that I would need the words from my baby to help me live my life without her?

Page 136

Chapter 16: Moving On Without Kelsey

Kelsey wrote this in one of her writings.

Romans 8:28 "All things work for the good of those who love the Lord, who are called according to His purpose." I know that life may seem unfair or challenging right now, but God has not forgotten you. This trial that you are experiencing will work for your good. You will come through this stronger. Think about this way...In order to have a rainbow, you must first have rain. I pray that God will give you the strength and courage to endure. I pray that you He will grant you your heart's desire. Just trust in Him, but while you are going through don't forget to praise Him for what you already have...you have life. You have the ability to even type your thoughts on this computer. You have eyes to see. You have been able to accomplish goals inspite of obstacles. There is power and praise...Don't give up and don't give in. God is not through with you yet.

This scripture has become one of my favorite scriptures. I believe there is a reason Kelsey went to be with God so soon. I know that she has touched more lives in her death than I think she would have had she lived. She has brought several of them to Christ in her death. Kind of like how she got closer to God after the death of Brett and Chucky. I can tell you that I am closer to God because of this. I could NOT live without Him in my life.

Ronnie and I have said, that if God came to us, Courtney, Kelsey, Ronnie, and I, and said, "I have to take one of you so the rest of you can be saved. Which one wants to come with me?" Kelsey would have been the one to raise her hand. I know that before Kelsey passed away, there is NO WAY I would have raised my hand. Ronnie has said the same. But we know that she would have gladly given her life for us, for anyone.

At the time of this writing it has been two years seven months and seventeen days since Kelsey passed away. Sometimes I feel like she is slipping away from me. Memories are fading. Maybe that is why I feel like I have to talk about her all the time. People tell me it will get easier with time. Hard to believe that. How can it be easy when half of your heart is broken? They say I will develop a "new norm." Well I don't want a "new norm." I want "my Norm!"

I see her friends and others going on with their lives. They have a full life ahead of them. But sometimes I get angry at them and even my family members. How can they be so happy? How can they move on? I certainly can't. I once had a 'perfect' life. A 'perfect' family. Now I live in what I call Hell. I know I have my Courtney and I love my

Courtney so, so much, but life without Kelsey isn't what I planned. Life without Kelsey isn't easy and I don't like it.

It's the things that happen that Kelsey should be here for. Like my niece giving birth to her first baby. A beautiful baby girl in September 2012. I was there when she was born. I had such mixed emotions. I was so happy for her and her husband. I was happy for my sister. She was a grandma for the first time. But at the same time I was mad. Kelsey should have been there. It wasn't fair that she wasn't there to celebrate the birth of Macey. I was angry that

Kelsey would never give me a grandchild. I was angry that Kelsey would never be married and know what true love was. It wasn't fair. How could this happen?

She should have been here for cousin, Joshua's, graduation from the State Police Academy. That day was a happy/sad day for me. I love Joshua and Natalie as if they were my own children. I was so happy and proud of Joshua. The nineteen weeks he was at the academy was very hard. Not just physically, but emotionally as well. We prayed that Josh would make it. I sent him Kelsey's favorite scripture,

Philippians 4:13, "I can do all things through Christ who strengthens me".

He made it. As we sat in the restaurant after graduation,

Kelsey should have been there.

I looked at Josh and said, "I haven't been this happy in ... I don't know how long." I told him Kelsey would be so proud of him and I wish that she was here to see this. I told him I knew she was looking down on him with a huge smile on her face saying, "I knew you could do it."

She should be here to be her sister's maid of honor. She should be here to get married and have babies. She should be here for me to yell at and tell her to straighten up or get a job, or study. She should be here to take care of her dad and me when we get old. She should be here!!!!

This is all the "human" part of me. The Christian part of me knows Kelsey is safe. She is happy in Heaven with God. She is the lucky one. She has no more worries. She doesn't shed anymore tears, and she doesn't have the weight of the world on her shoulders anymore. She is at peace. I "Believe" that one day, we will all be together again.

Mark 9:23 — And Jesus said to him, "If You can?' All things are possible to him who believes."

As I sit at her grave and listen to songs on my i-phone I think a lot of many different things. I lay there counting how many airplanes fly over us. I think of the people on those planes and wonder where they are going. I think, and I don't know why, here I am lying at my daughter's grave and they don't even know I exist. I look at the clouds trying to find some kind of sign from God that it will be okay. I look at the moon, when I am there at night, and pretend that is where Kelsey is. That she isn't that far from me. Just to the moon. But I know in my heart that isn't true. She is far away in Heaven with God.

There are several songs on my iPhone that I listen to. There are a couple in particular that I really like. One is by

Matthew West called "Save a Place for Me." The song is about his mother passing away and him telling her to save a place for him, he will be there soon. I tell Kelsey to save a place for me. Mommy will be there soon. I pray all the time that the Lord will come back soon like He said. That way my family will be back together and there will be no more pain. We will finally be "Home".

How does anyone survive this? How do we go on with our lives without our Kelsey? I can tell you, for me, it isn't easy. I know that without the help of God, my faith in Him, I could NOT do it. I don't know how people can even cope with the loss of a child without Him. Think about it; if you didn't believe in Heaven you would be thinking that you would never see your loved one again. How could you do that? I cannot wrap my brain around that. If I didn't believe in Heaven and wasn't able to look forward to seeing Kelsey again I would not survive.

Here is my belief and it is said perfectly in the scripture

Romans 8:28, "And we know that in all things God works for the good of those who love Him, who have been called according to His purpose".

Everyone has a purpose in life. I believe that mine, given to me by God, is to save as many lives as I can. Not only by spreading the word on the dangers of cell phone use and driving, but also "save lives" by telling Kelsey's story and spreading the word of God and how with Him there is eternal life. Leading people to Christ through Kelsey's story and how I became closer to God because of her death is my "purpose" in life.

I have never been mad at God for Kelsey's death. I know that she is in a safe place and she is at peace. I know a lot of people don't understand how I can't be mad at Him. He did take her, didn't He? Well, God never wants us to hurt or be sad. When we cry, He cries with us. He wasn't "teaching" me a lesson. God is a loving God. He sends angels to watch over us and to take care of us. Every time I am at Kelsey's grave and I am having a hard time, I can feel angels put their arms around me. I can hear someone telling me everything is alright and I feel a sense of peace. It isn't my imagination. It is God sending down angels to help me through this difficult time.

Proverbs 3:5 "Trust in the Lord with all your heart and lean not on your own understanding."

This scripture has become one of my favorites. I have to trust in Him that where He is leading me is what I am supposed to do. I do not understand why Kelsey was taken from us at such a young age, but what I do know is that I trust the Lord with all my heart. Ronnie and I have tried to figure out God's plan but it is really hard to do. I have said earlier in this book that if God sat Ronnie, Courtney, Kelsey, and myself down and told us that He had to take one of us so other lives, including ours, could be saved, Kelsey would have not hesitated one bit and she would have raised her hand and asked God to take her. I know that with all my heart. She would have given her life for us. What an amazing feeling to know that your daughter would give her life so you could be saved.

Don't get me wrong, I am human and I do have my days where I don't understand all this and I want my Kelsey back. Any human being would. I miss her so much my heart literally hurts. There are some days I don't even want to get out of bed. There are some days I just want to scream at the top of my lungs and punch the wall. There are times I am at her grave asking why? But I have to keep telling myself to trust in Him. That one day I will know why. I cannot wait for the day I am in Heaven with God and I get to hug my Kelsey once again. She had the best hugs. I will be "Home at Last".

I still sometimes wonder if she is happy and I know that is a silly thought, but it is the 'human' in me. The 'mommy' in me always wanting my girls to be happy.

But I believe. I Trust I have a purpose and I have strength. All because my daughter raised her hand.

In the summer of 2012 I received my answer. All summer I was seeing bluebirds at her grave. I thought that was odd as I had only seen maybe ten bluebirds in my entire life and over the course of that summer I had seen around thirty. One day in early fall, I was on my way to a presentation down state. I was by myself for this trip. When I am alone it's really hard on me because all I do is think about

Kelsey as I am driving. Needless to say, I am sad the whole time. I was about half way to where I was going when I noticed a bird up ahead on the side of the road. When I got close, close enough to see what kind it was, it started to fly away and I realized it was a bluebird. "What is with these bluebirds," I thought to myself. The next day I was back home and Ronnie and I went downtown shopping. There in a store was a little tree ornament. Yep you guessed it. A bluebird, but this bluebird had "Believe" written on it! I looked at Ronnie laughing and I said I don't get it. Why am I seeing all these bluebirds? I purchased the ornament. We left the store and Ronnie said, "Snow White." Snow White had bluebirds around her in the movie." I said, "That is it!" You see, Snow White was Kelsey's favorite Disney character. She slept in a snow white costume forever. She even wore it to her babysitters, my sister Lori's house. One day Lori caught Kelsey with her Snow White costume, on in the bathroom singing, "I'm wishing, for the one I love" into the toilet, as if it was a wishing well. Kelsey was only maybe three at the time.

Ronnie and I arrived at the next store. As we got to the check-out Ronnie stood in front of this display. He looked at me and said, "You are not going to believe this." He stepped aside. There was a display of some product and the name of the product? "Bluebird". I looked up to the sky and said, "Okay I got it." Ronnie proceeded to tell me, as we are on our way home, that bluebirds are the birds of happiness. So all summer long God had sent bluebirds to let me know that Kelsey is happy with him in Heaven. I praise God for sending me the sign and I'm sorry that it took me all summer to figure it out. But you know what? God didn't give up on it. He kept sending me bluebirds until I realized what he was trying to tell me. God loves us and he wants us to be happy and He NEVER gives up on us!

And we know that in all things God works for the good of those who love Him, who have been called according to His purpose. Romans 8:28

Kelsey Dawn Raffaele

May 2, 1992 – January 24, 2010

Made in the USA
Charleston, SC
09 February 2013